Curriculum Bank

KEY STAGE TWO
SCOTTISH LEVELS C-E

PHYSICAL EDUCATION

D1335286

GLENN BEAUMONT

Published by Scholastic Ltd,
Villiers House,
Clarendon Avenue,
Leamington Spa,
Warwickshire CV32 5PR
Text © Glenn Beaumont
© 1997 Scholastic Ltd
8 9 0   4 5 6

AUTHOR
GLENN BEAUMONT

EDITOR
JOEL LANE

ASSISTANT EDITOR
KATE PEARCE

SERIES DESIGNER
LYNNE JOESBURY

DESIGNER
LOUISE BELCHER

ILLUSTRATIONS
PETER STEVENSON

COVER ILLUSTRATION
JONATHAN BENTLEY

INFORMATION TECHNOLOGY CONSULTANT
MARTIN BLOWS

SCOTTISH 5–14 LINKS
MARGARET SCOTT AND SUSAN GOW

Designed using Aldus Pagemaker

British Library Cataloguing-in-Publication Data
A catalogue record for this book is available from the
British Library.

ISBN 0-590-53413-0

The right of Glenn Beaumont to be identified as the Author of this work
has been asserted by him in accordance with the Copyright, Designs
and Patents Act 1988.

All rights reserved. This book is sold subject to the condition that it
shall not, by way of trade or otherwise, be lent, hired out or otherwise
circulated without the publisher's prior consent in any form of binding
or cover other than that in which it is published and without a similar
condition, including this condition, being imposed upon the
subsequent purchaser.

No part of this publication may be reproduced, stored in a retrieval
system, or transmitted, in any form or by any means, electronic,
mechanical, photocopying, recording or otherwise, without the prior
permission of the publisher. This book remains copyright, although
permission is granted to copy page 78 and pages 104–157 for
classroom distribution and use only in the school which has purchased
the book and in accordance with the CLA licensing agreement.
Photocopying permission is given for purchasers only and not for
borrowers of books from any lending service.

Contents

ACKNOWLEDGEMENTS

The publishers gratefully acknowledge permission to reproduce the following copyright material:

Trafford Metropolitan Borough Council and Bob Merrell for ideas developed in Chapter 4 of this book from *Planning Dancing Lessons* by Lynda Cole © 1995, Trafford Metropolitan Borough Council.

Moonraker Productions and Mike Harding for the use of 'King Cotton' by Mike Harding from *A Bomber's Moon* © 1987, Mike Harding (1987, Michael Joseph Ltd).

Glenn Beaumont wishes to acknowledge the invaluable assistance and advice given by Janet Pritchard in compiling this book.

Introduction

Scholastic Curriculum Bank is a series for all primary teachers, providing an essential planning tool for devising comprehensive schemes of work as well as an easily accessible and varied bank of practical, classroom-tested activities with photocopiable resources.

Designed to help planning for and implementation of progression, differentiation and assessment, *Scholastic Curriculum Bank* offers a structured range of stimulating activities with clearly stated learning objectives that reflect the programmes of study, and detailed lesson plans that allow busy teachers to put ideas into practice with the minimum amount of preparation time. The photocopiable sheets that accompany many of the activities provide ways of integrating purposeful application of knowledge and skills, differentiation, assessment and record-keeping.

Opportunities for formative assessment are highlighted within the activities where appropriate, while separate summative assessment activities give guidelines for analysis and subsequent action. Ways of using information technology for different purposes and in different contexts, as a tool for communicating and handling information and as a means of investigating, are integrated into the activities where appropriate, and more explicit guidance is provided at the end of the book.

The series covers all the primary curriculum subjects, with separate books for Key Stages 1 and 2 or Scottish Levels A–B and C–E. It can be used as a flexible resource with any scheme, to fulfil National Curriculum and Scottish 5–14 requirements and to provide children with a variety of different learning experiences that will lead to effective acquisition of skills and knowledge.

PHYSICAL
EDUCATION

SCHOLASTIC CURRICULUM BANK PHYSICAL EDUCATION

The Scholastic Curriculum Bank *Physical Education* books help teachers to plan comprehensive and structured coverage of the physical education curriculum, and help pupils to develop the required skills and understanding through activities.

Each book covers one key stage. There is one book for Key Stage 1/Scottish Levels A–B and one book for Key Stage 2/Scottish Levels C–E. These books reflect the programmes of study for PE in the National Curriculum for England and Wales, and in the Scottish National Guidelines, with chapters addressing games, gymnastics, dance, athletics, outdoor/adventurous activities and swimming in Key Stage 2; and games, gymnastics and dance in Key Stage 1. Additional chapters refer to general considerations when teaching and assessing physical education.

Bank of activities

This book provides a bank of activities that can be used in two ways: to form a framework for a scheme of work, or to add breadth and variety to an existing scheme. The activities are designed to encourage children to develop as enthusiastic, responsive and knowledgeable performers in physical education.

Lesson plans

Detailed lesson plans, under clear headings, are given for each activity. They provide material which can be directly implemented in the appropriate space (the hall, playground, field, swimming baths and so on).

Activity title box

The information in the title box at the beginning of each activity outlines the following key aspects:

▲ *Activity title and learning objective.* Each activity has a clearly stated learning objective, given in bold italics. These learning objectives break down aspects of the programmes of study into manageable teaching and learning units, and their purpose is to aid planning for breadth and balance. They can easily be referenced to the National Curriculum and Scottish 5–14 requirements by using the overview grids at the end of this chapter (pages 9 to 12).

▲ *Class organisation/likely duration.* Icons †† and ⏰ signpost the suggested group sizes for each activity and the approximate amount of time required to complete it. Timing arrangements are by their nature arbitrary, as many factors are involved (including the children's previous skills and knowledge).

▲ *Health and safety.* Where necessary, health and safety considerations are flagged by the icon ▲. However, it is essential that checks be made as to what LEA regulations are in place.

Previous skills/knowledge needed

The information given here alerts teachers to particular knowledge or skills that the children will need prior to carrying out the activity.

Key background information

The information in this section is intended to set the scene and provide helpful guidance for the teacher. The guidance may relate to children's learning, to teachers' knowledge of physical education or to both.

Preparation

Advice is given for those occasions where it is necessary for the teacher to prepare the children for the activity or to collect and prepare materials ahead of time.

Resources needed

All the equipment, materials and photocopiable sheets needed to carry out the activity are listed here, so that the children or the teacher can gather them together easily before the beginning of the teaching session.

What to do

Easy-to-follow, step-by-step instructions are given for carrying out the activity, including (where appropriate) suggested points for discussion. Issues of playing area management are raised where relevant. In most cases, the activity plan is divided into phases incorporating a warm-up activity, a skill development activity and a conclusion.

Suggestion(s) for extension/support

Where possible, ways of providing for easy differentiation are suggested. Thus the lesson plans can be modified for less able pupils and extended for the more able.

Assessment opportunities

Each lesson plan has clearly-staged assessment opportunities which relate directly to the learning objectives for that activity and provide the framework for ongoing assessment. By taking advantage of these assessment opportunities, teachers can be reassured that the stated learning objectives have been covered.

Lesson allocations

The minimum number of lessons per week is three. In most cases, each lesson should be approximately 30 minutes long (excluding changing time). Some of the lesson plans in this book involve much longer sessions (for example, in chapter 6).

	Games	Gymnastics	Dance	Athletics	Outdoor and adventurous activities	Swimming
Year 3 (P4)	30 lessons	18 lessons	18 lessons	12 lessons	6 lessons	
Year 4 (P5)	30 lessons	18 lessons	18 lessons	12 lessons	6 lessons	
Year 5 (P6)	36 lessons	24 lessons	18 lessons	12 lessons	? lessons	24 lessons
Year 6 (P7)	36 lessons	20 lessons	24 lessons	12 lessons	? lessons	24 lessons

Figure 1

Opportunities for IT

Where opportunities for IT application arise, these are briefly outlined (on pages 158 to 160) with reference to particularly suitable types of program. The chart on page 160 lists specific areas of IT covered in the activities; the accompanying text provides more detailed guidance on how to apply particular types of program.

Reference to photocopiable sheet(s)

Where activities include photocopiable activity sheets, these are referred to in the lesson plans and can be found at the end of the relevant chapter.

Summative assessment

Each lesson plan presents advice on what the teacher should look for during the course of the lesson. A concluding chapter on assessment in physical education offers advice on how teachers might approach assessment in a summative way towards the end of a particular year or the key stage. Because the children's work in physical education will not primarily take the form of written or made products, it is suggested that the child's 'portfolio' for summative assessment purposes be built up in the form of records of achievement (including 'merit awards' for performance and effort, which could be taken from photocopiable pages 156 and 157).

Photocopiable activity sheets

Many of the activities are accompanied by photocopiable activity sheets. Some sheets may be used for assessment purposes – for example, those offered in aspects of outdoor/ adventurous activities or health-related activity. Other sheets are designed to help the teacher and children with the planning of certain activities, as in gymnastics. Some could be displayed around the working areas as aides-mémoire in helping the children to develop the technical aspects of their performance.

PE AT KEY STAGE 2

For the great majority of children physical education provides a rewarding and fulfilling part of school life, adding necessary balance to the more academic rigours of the 'classroom' curriculum. This is not to say, however, that physical education has no part to play in developing the intellect. PE will continually make intellectual demands upon the children in asking them to plan and evaluate their actions in a wide range of physical activities. Indeed, PE in Key Stage 2 of the National Curriculum is at its broadest, containing six different and contrasting activities: games, gymnastics, dance, athletics, outdoor/ adventurous activities and swimming – the sum total of which offers to children a complete and lasting physical experience. No single activity is capable of accomplishing this by itself.

Although physical education should always seek to be enjoyable, it is as much concerned with learning outcomes as any other aspect of the curriculum. One of the universal prime objectives of physical education is to make all children – irrespective of their natural ability – more skilful across a range of activities. PE is equally concerned with making children more knowledgeable about their own capacity for

Introduction

	Autumn Term		Spring Term		Summer Term	
Year 3 (P4)	Games Dance Athletics	Games Dance Swimming	Gymnastics Dance Swimming	Games Gymnastics Swimming	Games Gymnastics Swimming	Games OAA Athletics
Year 4 (P5)	Games Dance Athletics	Gymnastics Swimming Games	Dance Swimming Games	Dance Swimming Gymnastics	Games Swimming Gymnastics	Games OAA Athletics
Year 5 (P6)	Games Gymnastics Dance	Games Gymnastics Dance	Games Gymnastics Dance	Games Dance Gymnastics	Games OAA Athletics	Games OAA Athletics
Year 6 (P7)	Games Gymnastics Athletics	Games Gymnastics Dance	Games Gymnastics Dance	Games Gymnastics Dance	Games OAA Dance	Games OAA Athletics

Figure 2

movement and how it can be employed effectively to communicate and express. Health and fitness have always featured as major concerns within the PE curriculum. In Scotland, 'Investigating and developing fitness' and 'Using the body' are highlighted as strands of the PE Attainment Outcome 'Using materials, skills, techniques and media'. In short, the goals of physical education, as depicted in the requirements and guidelines of the various national curriculum documents throughout the United Kingdom, are wide-ranging and ambitious. Their achievement can make a significant and lasting contribution to the quality of life of all children.

Physical education in the primary school is concerned with establishing a broad foundation of skills and movement knowledge, upon which the more specialised secondary school programme can build. This places an enormous burden on the primary school teacher for without the benefit of an effective initial preparation, the progress of children through the increasing demands of more complex activities at secondary level will inevitably be compromised. This difficulty is further compounded by the fact that the majority of primary school teachers – however committed to the values of physical education and the physical development of their children – are not PE specialists, though many seek to enhance their expertise through regular attendance at in-service courses.

This Curriculum Bank seeks to assist primary school teachers in their effective teaching of physical education by not only providing progressive lesson material relating to the activities of PE, but also by discussing the nature of these activities and their unique contribution to the physical and psycho-motor development of children. The first chapter deals with the essentials of physical education, and covers the general requirements and common strands that characterise good teaching in any area of PE. Separate chapters are devoted to each of the six activities of the Key Stage 2 PE

curriculum. The final chapter offers guidance on assessment and record-keeping in PE.

Each chapter starts with an introduction which seeks to describe the nature of the activity concerned and the distinctive contribution that it makes to the overall physical development of children. Safety issues are also discussed. A structure for progression is suggested, which summarises the work to be covered over the four years of Key Stage 2. The main part of each chapter is a series of sample lessons, which reflect a suitable progression and indicate the kind of work that a typical class of children should be pursuing at various points in the key stage. In some cases (as in the 'Swimming' chapter), the lesson structure incorporates differentiation in terms of ability as well as progression in time.

Figures 1 and 2 will help the teacher in planning for overall curriculum balance by suggesting how many lessons may be appropriate for a particular activity (Figure 1) together with where it might be most effectively located within the key stage (Figure 2).

Learning objective	PoS/AO	Content	Type of activity	Page
The essentials of physical education				
To record patterns of exercise and determine whether this is sufficient activity for well-being.	KS1–4 1a, c *Investigating and developing fitness, level C*	**Understanding the ways in which the body responds to exercise** Physical activities to illustrate and give meaning to the concepts of strength, stamina and suppleness. Related classroom tasks involving basic anatomy and human biology.	Individual work. Group discussion. Recording using activity sheet.	18
To develop an understanding of the effects of exercise on the body, in particular on the heart and lungs.	As above *As above, level D*		Paired investigation. Group discussion. Recording. Data handling.	19
To develop understanding of the circulatory system.	As above *As above*		Group activity and discussion.	21
To understand that fitness consists of different elements, and that a range of activities are required to develop and maintain good general fitness.	As above *As above, level E*		Paired activity, group or class discussion. Individual activity sheets.	22
Games				
To develop sending and receiving skills using a large ball, with an initial emphasis on ball-handling. To improve spatial awareness and the ability to initiate and modify movement in a limited space.	1a, b, c *Using the body; Applying skills, level C*	**Skills, tactics and understanding required in invasion games** Skill practice to develop: – travelling with a ball; – controlling a ball; – sending a ball to a partner or team-mate. Defensive and attacking strategies within small-side competitive games.	Individual, paired and group work involving co-operation and competition. Making decisions.	26
To further develop sending and receiving skills using a ball, with particular emphasis upon ball handling. To develop tactical awareness in a simple competitive game. To encourage pupils to organise and regulate their own activity.	As above *As above*		As above.	27
To consolidate ball-handling and passing skills within the context of a fast-moving, small-side ball game. To develop knowledge and understanding of attacking and defensive strategies commonly used in invasion games.	As above *As above, level D*	**Skills, tactics and understanding required in striking and fielding games** Skill practice to develop: – striking a ball with a bat; – throwing a ball for accuracy; – catching and fielding a ball. Team activities involving batting and fielding skills.	As above.	29
To develop basic striking, fielding and throwing skills using a soft ball.	As above *As above, level C*		As above.	30
To consolidate and further develop batting, throwing, catching and fielding skills. To introduce team activities associated with striking and fielding games.	As above *As above*		As above.	32
To introduce and develop small-side competitive team games encompassing major elements of traditional striking/fielding games. To consolidate throwing skills, with a particular emphasis upon accuracy.	As above *As above, level D*	**Skills, tactics and understanding required in over-the-net games** Skill practice to develop: – striking a ball with accuracy over a barrier; – taking up positions for attacking and defending on a court.	As above.	34
To develop basic techniques associated with striking a ball over a barrier (the 'net'). To develop an understanding of continuity in net games ('the rally').	As above *As above, level C*		Individual and paired work involving co-operation and competition. Making decisions.	35
To consolidate striking skills over a net. To introduce competitive court play and develop an understanding of basic court tactics and strategies.	As above *As above*		As above.	36

PHYSICAL EDUCATION

Learning objective	PoS/AO	Content	Type of activity	Page
To reinforce a range of basic ball skills: dribbling, passing and striking. *To develop team and social skills in a competitive game situation.* *To exercise responsibility through devising an agreed scoring system and keeping score reliably.*	As above *As above, level D*	(See above.)	Group work involving competition between teams. Planning, organising and recording.	37
Gymnastics				
To develop selected individual actions around the theme of travelling without using the feet.	2a, b *As above, level B*	**Performing a wide range of gymnastic actions, displaying control and contrast, using the floor and apparatus** Movement tasks to develop: – weight-bearing and travelling skills using different body parts; – control of, and improvisation with, the body in flight; – working with a partner. **Linking a series of gymnastic actions into a complex movement sequence using the floor and apparatus** Movement tasks to develop sequence building, linking together combinations of similar and contrasting gymnastic actions.	Individual and partner work. Evaluation of own and others' work.	42
To develop sequence-making by linking 'unlike' actions: balances and rolls. To perform the Arabesque. To describe, compare and contrast other children's performances.	2a, b, c *As above*		Individual and partner work. Evaluation of own and others' work. Exploration of movement ideas.	43
To develop sequence-building further, using benches and mats. To consolidate apparatus handling skills.	As above *As above*		As above.	45
To be introduced to partner work. To develop co-operation skills. To develop evaluation skills: making comments on a partner's performance and suggesting appropriate improvements.	As above *Using the body; Applying skills; Observing and responding, level C*		Partner work. Evaluation of own and others' work. Exploration of movement ideas.	46
To encounter the concept of matching actions with a partner. To copy a partner's sequences, matching actions side by side and then one behind the other. To develop skills in copying identical actions and synchronising those actions. To practise taking weight on hands while kicking upwards.	As above *As above*		As above.	48
To further develop matched sequence work with a partner. To refine combinations of 1/4, 1/2 and 3/4 turns, and to include them in a sequence (either in a side-by-side formation or one behind the other). To devise a short sequence with a partner on medium-level apparatus.	As above *As above*		Individual, partner and group work. Evaluation of own and others' work. Exploration and refinement of movement ideas.	49
To explore the theme of balance further, using floor and apparatus. To explore different ways of moving into and out of balance. To link selected balances into free-flowing movement sequences.	As above *As above, level D*		As above.	51
To practise jumping skills from apparatus, focusing on resilient landings, elevation and extension in the air. To develop partner work skills further, using large apparatus.	As above *As above*		As above.	52
To practise jumping skills with a partner, synchronising take-offs and landings. To refine movement sequences with a partner, using large apparatus.	As above *As above*		As above.	54

PHYSICAL EDUCATION

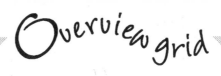

Learning objective	PoS/AO	Content	Type of activity	Page
Dance				
To explore, select and refine actions to make a dance with a clear beginning, middle and end. To interpret a poem, expressing mood and feeling through movement. To develop smooth linking of balances (see below) using turns and steps. To develop interpersonal skills through group work.	3a, c *Using the body; Creating and designing; Observing, describing and responding, level B*	Composing and performing simple dances using a range of auditory and visual stimuli Expressing mood and emotion through movement using poetry and a theme (the circus) as stimuli.	Individual, partner and group work. Exploration and refinement of creative movement. Planning, performing and evaluating.	58
To develop basic step patterns in dance, working to a simple rhythm. To create their own dances using a common step pattern.	3a, b, c *As above, level C*	Working with a partner and a group to synchronise and co-ordinate step patterns into a dance.	Individual and partner work, as above.	59
To develop travelling actions, with emphasis on stepping. To develop partner work skills, creating and performing dance patterns. To move in time to folk or traditional music that has a steady rhythm.	As above *As above*	Rhythmic reproduction of a range of step patterns associated with selected dances from various times and cultures	Individual, partner and group work, as above.	60
To gain experience of a dance from another culture: the French Stick Dance.	As above *As above, level D*	Practice, development and improvisation of basic folk and traditional step patterns to music.	Partner and group work, as above.	62
To select and combine basic actions to express characters based on the theme of a circus. To develop partner work skills of mirroring, leading and following and 'action-reaction'. To create a dance with a beginning, middle and end.	As above *As above, level D/E; Communicating, level D/E.*		Partner and large-group work leading to performance of a created and rehearsed dance sequence.	63
Athletics				
To develop running skills, with an emphasis on running quickly. To develop jumping for distance. To use opportunities for estimation and recording of athletic performance.	4a, b *Using the body; Applying skills; Co-operating and competing, level C*	Skill and understanding in running, jumping and throwing activities Skill practice to develop: – running for speed; – running over longer distances; – jumping; – throwing for distance; – relay baton exchange; – basic hurdling.	Partner and group work. Co-operative and competitive activity. Recording and evaluation of performance.	68
To develop running skills with an emphasis on conserving energy over longer distances. To develop throwing skills further, with particular emphasis on throwing a large ball for distance.	As above *As above*		Group work. Co-operative and competitive activity. Problem solving. Judging performance using simple rules. Recording and evaluating performance.	69
To become familiar with the baton relay race. To develop jumping skills further by combining jumps into a triple jump (hop, step and jump).	As above *As above*	Simple competition involving basic athletic activities.	Partner and group work, as above.	71
To further develop tactical running over longer distances. To further develop throwing a small ball and/or foam javelin for distance.	As above *As above, level D/E*	Judging and recording performance accurately across a range of basic athletic activities	Introductory group work in classroom. Partner and group work, as above.	72
To develop basic hurdling technique.	As above *As above*	Measuring and recording of personal performance using individual athletic record sheets.	Whole-class, group and paired work, as above.	74
To be involved in organising and carrying out a whole-school competitive activity. To build on the term's or year's work in PE. To observe and enforce rules of fair play.	As above *As above*		Group work involving competition between teams; judging, recording and handling data using record sheets.	75

PHYSICAL EDUCATION

Learning objective	PoS/AO	Content	Type of activity	Page
Outdoor and adventurous activities				
To be introduced to basic orienteering in the school grounds. To develop an understanding of how maps can be used as an aid to route finding. To develop teamwork and co-operation skills, and build self-reliance through decision-making.	5a, c *Applying skills, level D*	Skills, knowledge and understanding necessary to participate safely and with confidence in selected outdoor/adventurous activities	Group work. Planning. Making decisions. Recording using photocopiable page (PCP).	79
To work together in a group towards achieving a common goal. To undergo a series of 'adventure'-based problem-solving activities in order to develop their initiative and decision-making capability. To make imaginative use of the school grounds in creating an adventure environment.	5b, c *Creating and designing, level D*	Basic orienteering using the school grounds. Basic expedition preparation associated with the planning of, and responsible participation in, a low-level walk.	Group work. Making decisions. Problem solving and exploration. Discussion and evaluation of work.	80
To reinforce basic orienteering and problem-solving skills. To develop team co-operation skills further through competitive activity.	5a, b, c *Applying skills; Creating and designing, level D*	Personal and social skills necessary to respond effectively in a range of outdoor group problem-solving situations	Group work. Planning. Making decisions. Problem solving. Recording using PCP.	82
To be introduced to basic expedition work through a low-level walk. To develop the planning skills necessary for safe and responsible walking in the countryside.	5a, c *Applying skills, level D*	Participation in a variety of problem-solving activities around the school grounds.	Group and whole-class work. Planning. Making decisions. Exploration. Recording using PCP.	83
Swimming				
To be able to make a safe entry and exit into/out of water. To develop confidence in the water.	6b, d *Using the body; Applying skills, level C*	Water confidence and competence in the basic strokes of swimming	Teacher-directed individual and group work.	88
To continue building water confidence through jumping into the water and picking up objects from the pool floor and to learn the back crawl leg kick.	6b, c *As above*	Skill practices to develop: – effective stroke technique, propulsion and flotation; – swimming on the front and back; – swimming underwater.	Teacher-directed individual work.	89
To learn the breast stroke (full stroke). To practise underwater swimming.	6c *As above*		Teacher-directed individual and group work.	90
To learn push and glide techniques on the back. To complete a 10m swim on the back, using legs for propulsion.	6b, c *As above, level D*	Competence in the techniques and practices associated with water safety and survival	Teacher-directed individual work.	91
To understand the dangers associated with cold water immersion and develop the skills necessary to survive it.	6a, b, d *As above*	Skill practices to develop: – a range of water survival techniques (both individual and collective); – classroom work to develop knowledge and understanding of the effects of cold-water immersion on the body.	Teacher-directed individual work. Discussion.	93
To demonstrate a confident swim over 50m using front crawl, breast stroke and back crawl.	6a, c *As above*		Teacher-directed individual, paired and group work.	94
To learn the push and glide technique, on the back with arms extended. To swim 10m using back crawl.	6c *As above, level E*		Teacher-directed individual and group work.	95
To develop a fuller understanding of cold water survival in terms of energy conservation. To learn further skills to assist cold water survival.	6a, b, d *As above*		Teacher-directed individual and group work. Discussion.	97
To show good style in the swimming of front crawl, back crawl, breast stroke and butterfly.	6a, b, c *As above*		Teacher-directed individual and group work.	98

PHYSICAL
EDUCATION

The essentials of physical education

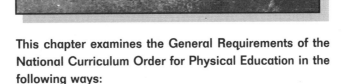

This chapter examines the General Requirements of the National Curriculum Order for Physical Education in the following ways:

▲ It seeks to clarify the meaning of 'performance' in physical education, so that teachers will be able to evaluate more effectively the quality of the response that children make to the range of physical challenges offered. This is taken further by relating selected teaching strategies and principles to aspects of skill and physical development.

▲ It suggests ways in which the activities themselves can contribute to the personal and social development of children.

▲ It offers a range of practical suggestions, in lesson form, designed to increase children's understanding of the effects of exercise on their bodies and how it promotes good health.

▲ It makes reference to some of the essentials associated with safe practice and how teachers can encourage a safe working environment in physical education.

The Scottish Guidelines for Expressive Arts 5–14 emphasise that 'it is within the context of engaging in physical activities that pupils develop creative responses, critical appreciation and interpersonal skills. They also experience and gain knowledge and understanding of the role of exercise in good health...' These principles are specifically addressed in this chapter, and then re-emphasised where appropriate throughout the activity-specific chapters.

PHYSICAL
EDUCATION

Entitlement for all pupils

The 1988 Education Reform Act, followed by the Revised Orders applying from September 1995, places a statutory obligation upon schools in England and Wales to make provision for the physical development of all pupils, irrespective of their aptitude and ability. The National Curriculum for Physical Education represents, for the first time within the state education system, a requirement for all pupils to be taught a range of activities which will:

▲ 'promote physical activity and healthy lifestyles';
▲ 'develop positive attitudes';
▲ 'ensure safe practice'.

(General Requirements for PE: Key Stages 1–4)

Similar qualities are sought within the Attainment Outcomes and Strands of the Scottish Guidelines for PE, though reference to safe practice is less explicit.

Although 'the greatest emphasis should be placed on the actual performance aspect of the subject', teachers will also need to ensure that pupils are directly involved in planning their activity and evaluating its outcome(s). Thus the teaching of PE goes far beyond mere 'physical' considerations associated with developing strong, supple limbs and stamina. It also needs to concern itself with helping pupils improve their knowledge and understanding of what makes for skilful and responsible participation. These qualities should be planned for in every PE lesson.

Planning, performing and evaluating

Developing performance in physical education is essentially a matter of **psycho-motor development**. In order to become more skilful – whether this involves throwing and catching a ball, performing a gymnastic sequence or swimming the length of a pool – all children need to think about their actions. They need initially to make decisions about what patterns of movement are required, for instance, to perform a given movement task or make a rapid response to a ball in flight – what might be called an **action plan**. Having decided what to do, they then need to co-ordinate the appropriate muscles and body parts so as to bring about the desired action in a smooth and fluent manner. When the action is completed, the children will need to make judgements about how effective their action has been: *Did it feel good? Was my shot on target? Did I include two balances in my sequence?* and so on. Of course, this entire process may sometimes have to be completed in a fraction of a second (as in a fast ball game, for example); but effective performance requires **thought as well as movement**, as the term 'psycho-motor' implies.

Practice, guidance and appropriateness

To help children successfully plan, perform and then evaluate their actions, the following teaching principles should prove useful:

1. *Pupils should be afforded regular practice sessions of sufficient duration.*

In planning and organising work in PE, it is necessary to ensure that appropriate amounts of time are made available for pupils to practise their skills and learn new ones. Although a small number of gifted children will be able to pick up new skills very quickly, the vast majority need to experience a new pattern of movement many times before their planning and evaluation of it begins to make sense to them.

When pupils achieve *consistency and intention* in performance, this is usually an indication that their learning has been effective. As a general rule, practice sessions which are short, intense and frequent are usually more productive in helping children to become more skilful than ones which are lengthy and irregular.

Psycho-motor skill performance involves much more than movement.

Skill is intentional.

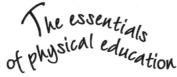

2. *Pupils need clear guidance.*

Although encouragement and praise are essential in maintaining the enthusiasm and motivation of pupils, it is equally important that children are given **technical** information that helps them to improve their performance. Ultimately, the children themselves will need to conceptualise the movement requirements of a new skill; but the teacher will need to assist this process with a few well-chosen observations. Feedback needs to be as precise as possible, focusing the children's attention on the crucial elements of the skill. It will sometimes be helpful to identify these key teaching points in lesson planning. However, too many teaching points can confuse the learner; two or three in each lesson are usually sufficient to provide a good basis for understanding.

3. *Pupils need appropriate physical challenges.*

From the time they start school to the end of Key Stage 2, the majority of children will have doubled their weight and increased in height by as much as fifty per cent. Thus, as Key Stage 2 progresses, children will tend to become more and more capable and confident in tasks which involve both strength and stamina. Significant improvement will usually be observed, for instance, in the performance of the basic skills: running, jumping and throwing. However, this improvement is not simply due to stronger muscles and more powerful lungs.

The **reaction time** of most children is significantly reduced over the two key stages: from about 0.6 secs for a typical Year 1/P2 child to 0.3 secs towards the end of Key Stage 2. This enables them to respond much more rapidly to a range of physical stimuli. The emerging ability of a Key Stage 2 child to adjust to the flight of a fast-moving ball and catch or strike it, provides a common example of this maturational development. Although most children from the ages of five to eleven tend to demonstrate similar patterns of physical and psycho-motor development, lesson material will always need to be sufficiently flexible to accommodate those children whose maturation rates are either faster or slower than the majority of their peers.

'Playing fairly and trying hard' – the contribution that physical education makes to personal and social development

By its nature, physical education provides abundant opportunities for children to develop a range of personal and social qualities. In the course of a typical PE lesson, children might be required to work in groups, or with a partner, in both co-operative and competitive contexts – in a game situation, for instance, or when setting out the large apparatus in gymnastics. At other times they will face individual physical challenges, possibly in swimming or when devising an appropriate movement to take them over a bench. The activities alone, however, are not generally sufficient to

Watch the ball! Stay on your toes! Move quickly... Look for space...

Avoid giving too many teaching points at once.

establish accepted and desirable codes of behaviour (which are hopefully transferable to other areas of life). The teacher must constantly seek to reinforce, and reward, behaviour which demonstrates perseverance, tolerance and thought for others (among other qualities), while disappproving of unsocial action and casual attitude.

The following teaching principles may be useful in establishing an appropriate framework for the PE lesson within which pupils are able to assimilate and value the importance of others while giving of their best.

Games

▲ When involving children in a competitive activity, try to make sure that the competitors or teams are well-matched in terms of their overall abilities.

▲ Make sure that the rules governing the activity are simple and are clearly understood and agreed on by all participants, thereby encouraging compliance and respect.

▲ Involve all pupils at some point in officiating and regulating their own activity.

▲ Emphasise the importance of praise and encouragement for peers and team-mates, while discouraging destructive criticism and blame.

▲ Pupils should be encouraged to compete fairly; to win if they can; to accept losing in good spirit; and ALWAYS to acknowledge the efforts of opponents.

Gymnastics

▲ All children should be involved in apparatus handling; co-operation between pupils, in the interests of everybody's safety, will be essential in lifting heavier pieces of equipment, such as mats, benches, and boxes.

▲ In carrying out a movement task, pupils will often be required to move freely around the floor and upon apparatus. They should be encouraged to take account of others in planning their own movements and adjust their actions if necessary.

▲ Although demonstration will be used primarily to assist learning and improve movement quality, it should also be used (on occasion) to display the work of the less able in a positive light, particularly in terms of noticeable effort.

Dance
▲ Pupils should be encouraged to value the efforts of other children in seeking to express mood and feeling. An atmosphere of mutual acceptance and support among the children will inevitably lead towards better and less inhibited performance.

Athletics
▲ In order to encourage individual effort, pupils should be given the opportunity to work towards and to value their own individual performance targets in addition to direct competition with their peers.
▲ Measuring and recording their own performance and that of their peers will help pupils to develop a sense of being responsible and trustworthy.

Outdoor and adventurous activities
▲ Pupils will need to experience both a leadership role and that of a group member. Less assertive children may need the sensitive support of their teacher when leading.
▲ In outdoor group problem-solving tasks, it is important that all pupils contribute in some way and each pupil is actively involved in finding solutions.
▲ Care for the environment will need to underpin all outdoor activity.

Swimming
▲ Of all the activities within the PE curriculum, swimming is probably the most highly structured. Children usually have before them a clear and graduated progression from beginner to advanced performer, often linked to a system of awards and badges. This provides a valuable opportunity for pupils to exercise longer-term goals and sustained effort, provided that the requirements of progression from one award to the next are reasonably demanding but seen by pupils to be achievable.
▲ Much of the programme in swimming will focus on water safety, including rescue. This will encourage qualities associated with individual responsibility, stressing the need to watch out for others, and, if necessary, to come to their assistance.

The importance of safety
All primary school physical education policies should contain a section on safety. This should include clear procedures for identifying children with health problems. It should also contain guidance about the necessary steps to be taken in the event of an accident. The five statements included in section 3 of the General Requirements in the PE National Curriculum for England and Wales provide a useful starting point in drawing up a safety policy to alert teachers and pupils to the need for safe practice.

It should be remembered that all schools are in *loco parentis* and that while the school is in session, this responsibility operates regardless of time, date or place. While in *loco parentis*, teachers are required to exercise a duty of care acceptable to a reasonable parent or guardian. This duty of care cannot be delegated. Because of the greater risk levels in physical education relative to other subjects, a higher duty of care is placed upon the PE teacher necessitating a certain accepted level of expertise and training.

A safe teaching environment exists when both the teacher and the pupils display a good understanding of safe practice. The following procedures relate to the responsibilities of the teacher, and would provide the basis for enquiry in cases of alleged negligence:

PHYSICAL
EDUCATION

1. All reasonable steps had been taken to ensure the safety of the premises and the equipment.

2. The class had been taught about the need for safety, and been warned against risk-taking, in a manner appropriate to the pupils' age, intelligence and experience.

3. The class had been systematically prepared for the activities being undertaken, and attention had been paid to footwear and clothing.

4. The work and the manner in which it was done were in keeping with regular and approved practice in other schools in the country.

5. Any local or overseas visits, outdoor pursuits or other occasional activities had proceeded with the prior agreement of parents/guardians by means of signed forms of consent.

In order for pupils to be taught effectively about safe practice it remains essential that:

▲ There is an orderly working environment in which control and concentration are maintained.

▲ Teachers and pupils work to a consistent framework throughout the school, whereby an understanding of safety procedures and responsible participation is reinforced on a regular basis.

▲ Appropriate clothing and footwear are worn, and the wearing of jewellery is strongly discouraged when children are participating in PE. The issue of jewellery which has religious significance should be approached sensitively. For example, be aware that Sikh boys will often wear a steel bangle called a *kara* which they will not want to remove. Suggest that they hold it in place and avoid hurting others with it by covering it with a towelling sweatband. Some children may also need to wear items for health reasons, such as Medi-Alert bracelets; again, these should be securely attached and covered to prevent accidents. Wherever possible, teachers should set a good example and at the very least change their footwear for PE lessons.

▲ Pupils are given responsibility for setting out their own equipment and apparatus, but are provided with clear instructions and guidance about its safe management by the teacher.

Two further observations serve to reinforce the above. Firstly, primary teachers will know their pupils well. In addition to a comprehensive understanding of the intellectual/ academic capabilities of individual pupils, they also acquire insights into pupils' emotional/behavioural characteristics – for example, which children are naturally cautious or more adventurous. Such knowledge frequently proves valuable in making judgements about the appropriateness of an activity or physical situation to particular children.

Secondly, the importance of **progression** within the context of safety (as well as the context of effective learning) cannot be emphasised too strongly. Where pupils have been allowed the opportunity to establish foundation skills firmly before being encouraged or guided towards more complex and difficult actions – for example, developing control when jumping on the floor before being introduced to platforms – the risk of accident is drastically reduced.

More specific guidance on safety is given with each activity chapter. It is also strongly recommended that every school acquires a copy of *Safe Practice in Physical Education* published by The British Association of Advisers and Lecturers in Physical Education (1995). This comprehensive book provides teachers with safety guidance on all aspects of physical education, and is recognised by the DFEE as the definitive work on safety in PE.

Physical activity and health

The lessons and activities described on pages 19–22 will help children to explore the anatomical and physiological basis of exercise, while helping them towards a better understanding of physical fitness and its contribution to health. They are not necessarily progressive activities, and you will need to identify (as part of your key stage curriculum planning) the best time to deliver them, for example to link with relevant work in science.

THE EXERCISE DIARY

To record patterns of exercise and determine whether this is sufficient activity for well-being.

†† *Individual work.*

🕐 *10 minutes per day, followed by 30-minute group discussion.*

Previous skills/knowledge needed

The children should have the ability to record and analyse simple data.

Key background information

Although there is no hard evidence that the children of today are any less healthy or fit than their predecessors of, say, forty or fifty years ago, it can certainly be said that many features of modern living predispose children towards a sedentary lifestyle. Clearly, advances in health care and nutrition have reduced the incidence of many childhood illnesses; but a nagging doubt remains that many children are often denied the opportunity to exercise frequently and vigorously enough to support the process of healthy growth and maturation. The 'Exercise diary' (photocopiable sheet 104) will help the class to record their normal patterns of exercise over a typical week, and will help to generate discussion about the amount and types of exercise that are considered beneficial to the children's well-being.

Preparation

Before the lesson, engage the class in a discussion about health and exercise. General points that need to emerge include:

▲ Exercise needs to be taken frequently to assist good health – at least three sessions of moderate/vigorous exercise per week of about 20 minutes' duration.

▲ Different types of activity develop different aspects of overall fitness.

▲ Sustained, continuous activity such as running, cycling or swimming will develop stamina; climbing, hanging, heaving and weight-bearing activities help to build strength; suppleness will be maintained through activity that involves stretching and wide-ranging movement.

▲ Warm-up actions before exercise commences and cool-down actions after it has finished are important. The emphasis should be upon gentle stretching movements involving the major joints. Warm-ups and cool-downs help muscles and joints to prepare for and recover from exercise, thereby minimising the risk of injury.

▲ Good hygiene when exercising usually involves changing into and out of PE kit.

Resources needed

A range of basic reference books about health and exercise, one copy per child of photocopiable sheet 104.

What to do

Give each child a copy of the 'Exercise diary' (photocopiable sheet 104) one Monday afternoon. Encourage them to spend ten minutes each day writing in what exercise they did that day and when. You may need to remind the children that walking to school or running for the bus are also forms of exercise.

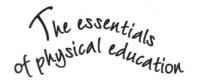

At the end of the week, ask them to add up the total amount of exercise time and determine what form of exercise they did most of. They should analyse how the different types of exercise may have helped their bodies. Refer back to any earlier discussion and direct them to any useful reference books you have available. It may also be useful to ask the children to compare their own lifestyles with those of their parents or grandparents, in order to highlight the differences in exercise patterns and the potentially sedentary nature of modern living.

Suggestion(s) for extension
More able children could compare their own weekly activity with the training schedules of professional athletes, dancers and so on.

Suggestion(s) for support
Children who have poor numeracy and literacy skills should be encouraged to record their exercise activity on audio tape.

Assessment opportunities
Observe how conscientiously the children complete their diaries. Are they able to match times of day to the activities? Are they able (and willing) to analyse critically the amount and type of exercise they have?

Reference to photocopiable sheet
Photocopiable sheet 104 provides a format for the children's recording of their exercise in one week and some analysis of that data in terms of its relevance to developing fitness.

CHART OF THE HEART

To develop an understanding of the effects of exercise on the body with particular reference to the heart and lungs.

†† *Children working mostly in pairs.*

🕐 *Drawing activity 30 minutes; physical exercise and recording 20 minutes; discussion 10 minutes.*

Previous skills/knowledge needed
The children need the ability to work co-operatively (in pairs or small groups), and to record and interpret simple data. They should know how to locate the radial pulse (in the wrist) and measure it.

Key background information
Many pupils are unsure of the location, shape and size of their heart and lungs. This lesson will help to clarify their knowledge and will lead to interesting discussion. For example, the heart of a child is about the size of the child's fist, situated more or less in the middle of the chest; the lungs are situated on either side, each three or four times as big as the heart, and almost in the shape of a right-angled triangle. If the lungs were unravelled, the flattened lung tissue would cover a tennis court!

Working muscles cannot operate for long without a steady supply of oxygen. Oxygen is taken into your body by your lungs. The oxygen is transferred to the blood, which is then pumped by the heart around the body. During exercise, the heart rate will increase; some forms of exercise make the heart work harder than others. For example, press-ups involve local muscle strength in the arms and do not require too much heart/lung involvement. A gentle stretching and bending warm-up involves only a little more heart/lung

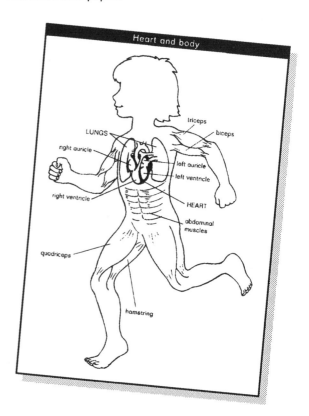

locate their radial pulse (in the wrists) and count it over a 15-second period. Tell them to multiply this number by four to convert it to beats per minute.

Now tell them, working in pairs, to do as many press-ups as they can in 30 seconds and then have their partners check their heart rates. They should record, change roles and repeat the task. Then they should do some easy bending and stretching exercises for two minutes. After the prescribed time, they should check their partner's heart rate, record it, change roles and repeat.

Next, the children should either jog around the playground without stopping too frequently for five minutes, or, alternatively step briskly up and down onto and off a low bench for five minutes. They should check their partner's heart rate immediately on stopping and record it; then reverse roles and repeat.

Finally, each pair should join with another pair and discuss: *Which activity produced the highest heart rate? Why?* They should write down their answers and compare them with the findings of the rest of the class. The children should conclude that activity which is sustained and involves the whole body raises the heart rate the most.

Suggestion(s) for extension
Ask the children to plot everybody's heart rate graphically and look for differences between the girls' and boys' results. Can the children find any differences? (There should not be any.)

Suggestion(s) for support
Try to pair children who have literacy/numeracy difficulties with more able pupils.

activity. A sustained activity such as jogging or skipping, involving the large skeletal muscle groups, raises the heart rate significantly since the harder-working muscles require a more plentiful supply of oxygen.

Preparation
The teacher may find it useful to make a simple, large-scale (but reasonably accurate) drawing of the basic anatomy of the body, showing particularly the location of the heart, the lungs and some of the larger skeletal muscles. The positions of these organs are shown on photocopiable sheet 105, which could be photoenlarged and coloured appropriately.

Resources needed
Large sheets of paper, big enough for a child to lie on, felt-tipped pens or crayons in different colours; low benches; a large working area such as the hall or playground; stopwatches; basic reference books or charts on human anatomy and physiology, showing the respiratory organs; one or more enlarged copies of photocopiable sheet 105 for the teacher's and/or children's reference.

What to do
In the classroom or hall, ask the children to draw around a partner, producing a body silhouette on the paper. Ask the children to draw in (with pens or crayons) where they think the heart and lungs are situated, and their approximate size and shape. Prepare yourself for a few surprises! Suggest that the children use the reference books available to check their ideas about these organs.

Now involve the children in some practical work in the hall involving exercise and heart rate. First of all, ask them to measure and record their **resting heart rate**. This is best done sitting down (on a low bench). The pupils should then

PHYSICAL EDUCATION

Assessment opportunities

Observe how accurately (in terms of size and location) the children draw the heart and lungs.

Reference to photocopiable sheet

Photocopiable sheet 105 is a diagram of the human lungs, heart and major skeletal muscles. Enlarged copies of this can be used by the teacher or the children as a resource in work on the effects of exercise on heart rate.

THE CIRCULATION RELAY

To develop understanding of the circulatory system.
†† *Children working mostly in groups of 5 or 6.*
🕐 *Warm-up jogging and stretching 5 minutes; relay activity 25 minutes; discussion 5–10 minutes.*

Previous skills/knowledge needed

The children need to have a basic knowledge of the functions of the heart, lungs and muscles.

Key background information

Although pupils will have developed their knowledge of the separate functions of the heart, lungs and muscles at an early point in Key Stage 2, the interdependence of these various organs in the transportation of oxygen is not always understood at this level. *The demand for 'fuel' (oxygen) increases as our bodies are required to do more work.* That simple statement provides the basis for a sound understanding of the effects of exercise on the body and how it adjusts its systems to meet different demands. The 'Circulation relay' diagram in Figure 1 demonstrates this process, and will help to consolidate the children's understanding of it.

Preparation

You will need to prepare a set of six large illustrated cards: one representing the lungs, one representing the muscles and four representing the four chambers of the heart.

Resources needed

Bean-bags (red and blue); skittles; cards (see 'Preparation'); playground or hall.

What to do

Set out the running circuit shown in Figure 1. Leave the cards identifying the major organs involved in blood circulation face down. Ask the children to transport the red and blue beanbags in specific sections of the circuit and deposit them with their respective 'collectors' – only red beanbags must be carried on certain sections of the course, and only blue ones on others. After a few minutes of continuous activity, reveal the cards to the children. Briefly discuss how the running circuit resembles their own circulatory system, with particular reference to the

colour of the beanbags (red represents oxygenated blood whereas blue represents deoxygenated blood).

Further activity may be provided by asking a pupil or small group to stand in the middle and perform a series of actions, such as running alternately quickly and slowly on the spot. The rest of the class moving around the circuit – representing blood in the arteries and veins – then have to adjust their speed in replicating the circulatory system's response to exercise: the more vigorous the activity in the middle, the faster they run. Change the group in the middle, so that every group has a turn. After each group has occupied the middle, ask the class the following question:
▲ *Which organ or system do you think the group in the middle represents?*
Hopefully the children will conclude that the middle group represents the brain or the central nervous system, which has the role of 'commanding', directing and co-ordinating all organic activity.

Suggestion(s) for extension

Introduce more complex terms, such as 'cardio-vascular system', into the discussion, together with a more detailed diagram of the heart (showing the atria and ventricles). Make the distinction between the blood flowing from the heart to the lungs and the blood flowing from the heart to the muscles, in terms of oxygen content.

Suggestion(s) for support

Make sure that drawings accompany the words on the cards used in the relay.

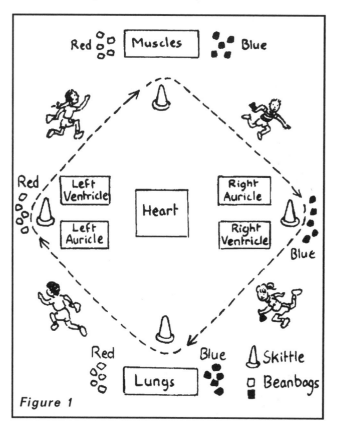

Figure 1

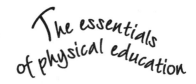

KEEPING FIT

To understand that fitness consists of different elements, and that a range of activities are required to develop and maintain good general fitness.

†† *Pairs or small groups.*

🕐 *Warm-up (jogging and stretching) 5 minutes; practical work 25 minutes; completion of task sheet 15–20 minutes.*

Preparation
Photocopiable activity sheets are included for this lesson; reading ability will determine which sheet(s) is/are given to each child. The number of copies to be prepared will thus depend on the relative sizes of the different ability groupings.

Resources needed
A marked area on the field or playground providing a 40m by 40m running circuit; tape measures; stop-watches; copies of photocopiable sheet 108 (for extension) and sheets 106 and 107 (for support).

Key background information
The six areas of activity in the PE National Curriculum – games, gymnastics, dance, athletics, outdoor/adventurous activity and swimming – will all contribute towards overall fitness, but in different ways. Games, for instance, will emphasise stamina, whereas gymnastics will be more concerned with strength and suppleness.

What to do
Begin with a warm-up of gentle jogging and stretching exercises. Then divide the class into pairs or small groups. Each pair should try all three activities:

1. Try to jog continuously, without stopping, for ten minutes around the running circuit.

2. Sit on the floor with your legs on the ground stretched out straight in front of you. Reach carefully forward with your fingertips and try to touch your toes. Keep the backs of your legs against the floor and move slowly – stop when it becomes uncomfortable. Can you reach your toes easily?

3. Stand on a line with your feet close together. Bend your knees and jump as far as you can. Swing your arms upwards to help you lift into the air and land in a still position. This is known as a **standing broad jump.** *Your partner will measure the distance you have jumped, from the line to the back of your heels. Take several jumps and then change over. Now measure your height. Can you jump a horizontal distance which is at least half of your height?*

The three activities the children have completed will have made different demands upon their bodies. Discuss with them how comfortable they felt when they were doing the exercises. How did their bodies respond to the activity? Was one activity easier for them than the other two activities?

Suggestion(s) for extension
More confident readers should complete photocopiable sheet 108.

Suggestion(s) for support
Less confident readers will be more effectively challenged by photocopiable sheets 106 and 107.

Assessment opportunities
The completed photocopiable sheets which accompany this lesson provide useful material for assessing children's knowledge and understanding of exercise and its effects on fitness.

Reference to photocopiable sheets
Photocopiable sheet 108 can be used for extension; it asks children to write about the effects of exercise on strength, stamina and suppleness. Sheets 106 and 107 can be used for support; they ask similar questions to sheet 108, but give pictorial multiple-choice answers.

Games

Games are played at all the key stages of the National Curriculum in England and Wales, and are seen as a 'core' activity in Scotland. Children are required to experience a range of games at Key Stage 2. These fall into three categories. In **invasion games** such as soccer or netball, the objective is to 'invade' your opponents' 'territory' with the ball in order to score a goal. In the primary school, the goal may be in the form of a skittle or hoop. **Striking and fielding games** match a batter against a number of fielders, who try to prevent the batter from scoring runs or rounders by quickly retrieving the ball or getting the batter 'out'. **Over the net** (or **against the wall**) **games** involve a 'court' divided by a net (or ending at a wall), over (or against) which players seek to hit a ball or other object in a way that makes it difficult for opponents to hit it back.

Whatever the game, teachers should ensure that children experience maximum involvement. This often means modifying the game in terms of the numbers playing, or using simple rules and scaled-down equipment to match the capabilities of the children and their stage of development. This chapter outlines a number of ways in which this might be achieved, making the early games experience of children an effective foundation for enjoyable and rewarding games playing in later years.

The lessons suggested for games reflect the requirements of the National Curriculum. Three lessons are presented for each type of game: invasion, striking/fielding and net/wall games. Although each lesson may

the ability to track a ball and predict its path with accuracy would seem to represent an aspect of performance which all ball games (to which the National Curriculum at Key Stage 2 specifically refers) include – there are, nevertheless, considerable differences between the concepts and skill demands involved in playing an invasion game such as football or hockey and those associated with a striking/ fielding game such as rounders or a net/wall game such as tennis. This will need to be considered in the planning and organisation of the primary games curriculum in order to maintain balance and progression.

All games require participants to **make decisions**, sometimes very rapidly (as in a fast ball game). The process by which the player uses information to initiate a response is illustrated below. As children progress through Years 1 to 6 (P2 to P7), their ability to undertake more complex decision-making across a range of games activities becomes apparent. This is partly due to the process of maturation, but is also dependent upon the quality of teaching. Thus, whatever the type of game, an effective teaching progression will seek to make more and more demands upon the children's capacity to decide what to do in particular game situations. The diagram below illustrates the decision-making sequence. It shows just a few of the many decisions a child will have to make in playing even a relatively simple ball game.

be used in its own right, their main purpose is to illustrate what might constitute suitable activity at the beginning, middle and end of Key Stage 2. The Key Stage Progression guide on page 25 will assist the teacher in long-term planning for games over the four years.

Additionally, the photocopiable task sheets provided may be used to emphasise and consolidate the main teaching points associated with a particular lesson or as warm-up activities. (The warm-up activities generally contain an element of basic training as well as helping to maintain fitness and prevent injury.) The photocopiable sheets (enlarged where possible) should be displayed clearly around the working area, either stuck to the wall or on cards attached to skittles. A further photocopiable sheet provides a framework for children to devise and organise their own sports event – this is a useful means of consolidating a range of games skills, on two or three occasions a year, in an enjoyable and competitive way.

Skill demands in games

The National Curriculum for England and Wales Programme of Study in Games and the Scottish 5–14 Guidelines require that children be taught a number of different games, each with its own particular skill requirements. Although some elements are common across different games – for instance,

Safety in primary games
General considerations

▲ Clothing should be appropriate to the game being played and the weather conditions.

▲ Footwear should be suitable. Playing any game on a wet and slippery grass surface necessitates a studded or well-ribbed sole. Beware of plastic soles, which quickly lose their grip and become hazardous. When playing competitive indoor games, discourage children from participating in bare feet since this affects both safety and hygiene.

▲ Jewellery should not be worn. (However, see the note on page 17 about religious observance and health-related items.)

▲ Orderly behaviour should be maintained, and children should be taught to respect each other and the rules of the game. They should be encouraged to adopt responsible attitudes in terms of their own safety and the safety of others, and to maintain a safe working environment. Chewing should not be allowed during participation in games.

Decisions to make when playing ball games

What is happening around me?	→	What action do I need to take?	→	What muscles do I need to move?
Where are my team-mates? Where are my opponents? Who has possession of the ball?		Where should I run to receive a pass? Who should I pass to? Where do I run to intercept a pass?		Am I required to kick, throw, catch, strike the ball? Do I need to stretch, jump, turn, run?

Games

Physical considerations
▲ Equipment and facilities should reflect the children's stage of development.

▲ Games equipment should be suitably scaled to reflect the strength, stamina and skill level of the children. Remember that skill levels deteriorate when children become fatigued. Be vigilant in making sure that the children do not exceed their capabilities.

Venues and working areas
▲ Ensure that working areas are free from obstructions and hazards. It is good practice, for instance, for the whole class to 'sweep' outdoor playing areas visually before commencing activities. Anything spotted by the children should be reported to the teacher and not handled by them. When working indoors, make sure that the nature of any competitive activity reflects the limitations of space.

Equipment
▲ Equipment should be regularly inspected and maintained. Games equipment, particularly large or heavy items such as goalposts, should be safely stored. All large free-standing equipment should be made secure.

▲ It is good practice, when playing striking and fielding games, to encourage the children to place their bats in a designated area (such as a hoop) rather than just dropping them. Whenever an activity is taking place, ensure that all items of equipment not currently being used are stored in a safe position, well away from the participants.

Key Stage progression
Games should be taught throughout the key stage on a regular basis, such as weekly for at least two terms per year. Over the key stage, pupils will progress from simple games to more demanding mini-versions of complex traditional games, but will continue to need time and opportunity to practise and consolidate the basic skills involved with sending, receiving and travelling with a ball (either individually or in pairs/small groups).

Years 3 and 4 (P4 and P5)
Invasion
▲ Development of sending (passing) and receiving (controlling) on the move with a partner.

▲ Competition introduced in sending and receiving games which emphasise retaining a team's possession of the ball such as 'piggy in the middle' activities with 3 against 1 or 4 against 2 – 'How many passes can you make before an interception occurs?'

Striking/fielding
▲ Emphasis upon striking, throwing, rolling and catching with a partner over short distances.

▲ Small-side rounders/cricket type games with 'guaranteed' batting time and individual scoring in a 'one versus the rest' format, such as one bowler, two fielders, one striker.

▲ Pupils given opportunities to develop striking skills using a range of different bats such as round wooden bats, plastic cricket bats and so on.

Over the net/against the wall
▲ Emphasis upon consistent striking against walls/rebound surfaces and sustained (co-operative) rallying with partner.

Years 4 and 5 (P5 and P6)
Invasion
▲ Consolidation and extension of sending and receiving a ball; introduction and development of travelling skills such as bouncing, carrying or dribbling a ball.

▲ Small-side games (such as 3 versus 3) to incorporate travelling skills and directional, point-scoring play, for example scoring goals, hitting skittles, carrying ball over opponents' line.

Striking/fielding
▲ Throwing and catching with partner over greater distances, with emphasis upon quick, accurate returns.

▲ Small-side (3 versus 3) rounders/cricket games.

Over the net/against the wall
▲ Introduction of a 'court' into 'over the net' games.

▲ Increasing emphasis upon competitive rallies.

Years 5 and 6 (P6 and P7)
Invasion
▲ Increased team numbers (but no more than 5 versus 5) to include mini-games of football, hockey, rugby, netball.

Striking/fielding
▲ Mini-games of cricket/rounders, but no more than 5 versus 5.

Over the net/against the wall
▲ Emphasis upon competitive rallying using small courts; introduction of doubles play.

INVASION GAMES –
Y3 & Y4 (P4 & P5)

To develop sending and receiving skills using a large ball, with an initial emphasis on ball-handling.
To improve spatial awareness and the ability to initiate and modify movement in a limited space.
†† *Paired warm-up activity; individual and paired skill development; game in groups of 6.*
🕐 *Warm-up 5 minutes; individual skill development 10 minutes; paired skill development 15 minutes.*

Previous skills/knowledge needed
The children should be able to throw, bounce and catch a ball, with reasonable consistency and control, when working individually. They should be able to work co-operatively, and to move safely in a crowded space.

Key background information
The response (reaction) time of early Key Stage 2 children is still maturing. The speed with which a seven-year-old reacts to the complex events of a competitive team game is limited by the time it takes her/him to make sense of the information arriving. Thus a fast ball game will present too many difficulties for most pupils. Activities in which the direction of the ball remains fairly predictable, with opposition kept at a minimal level, will provide an appropriate challenge.

The following key teaching points will be useful:
▲ *Always try to catch the ball with two hands – fingers spread wide.*
▲ *Watch the ball move into your hands.*
▲ *Keep your feet comfortably apart for good balance when catching and passing the ball. Stay on your toes when moving about space.*
▲ *Use both hands for control when passing the ball.*

Preparation
If it is practical, enlarged copies of photocopiable sheet 109 could be displayed around the working area (for example, on cards placed in the tops of skittles) to remind pupils about the main features of the activity.

If there are no floor markings available, indicate the working area with skittles.

Resources needed
One large, light ball for each child (vinyl-covered foam balls are effective here, particularly for indoor work); a suitably marked working area such as the hall or playground (try to avoid windy days if working outside); photocopiable sheet 109.

What to do
Warm-up activity
Start with a running/chasing game. Organise the class into pairs: one child is the 'marker' and the other is the 'dodger'. The aim is for the 'dodger' to keep as far away from the 'marker' as possible in 30 seconds' continuous activity, staying within the working area at all times. The children then swap roles. Encourage lots of stops and starts with changes of direction and pace by the 'dodgers'. Stress the need for all participants to watch out so that collisions are avoided.
Skill development
Ask the children to choose a ball and start with a whole-class individual activity based on photocopiable sheet 109.

Now ask the children to return to their partners and stand five strides apart, then practise passing the ball by throwing it with both hands underarm (from below the waist), from the chest (a 'push' pass) and then from overhead (a soccer throw). They should try to complete ten passes of each kind. Then make the activity competitive by asking which pair can be the first to complete ten passes without dropping the ball.
Game activity
Organise the children into groups of six. Five children make a circle of about five strides' diameter. The sixth child remains in the centre of the circle and attempts to intercept the ball

as the others pass it across or around the centre. Change the 'chaser' at regular intervals.

The partner and group activities described above could be modified in subsequent lessons to include kicking skills and work with small plastic hockey sticks.

Suggestion(s) for extension

For children requiring greater challenge:

▲ Put two 'chasers' in the middle of the circle and only allow passing *across* the circle; and/or

▲ After each pass, the passer must complete a run around the circle and back to her/his place as quickly as possible.

Suggestion(s) for support

For children experiencing difficulty:

▲ Allow the children to practise passing around the circle without a chaser in the middle. Set them a target of so many passes in one minute.

▲ Put a chaser in the middle but allow the chaser to move her/his arms only.

Assessment opportunities

Look for consistency in passing and receiving skills. Are the children beginning to make effective decisions about where and when to pass the ball by first observing the positions and movement of the chaser?

Reference to photocopiable sheet

Sheet 109 contains three activity cards which should be used to prompt the children's individual skill development.

INVASION GAMES – Y4 & Y5 (P5 & P6)

To further develop sending and receiving skills using a ball, with particular emphasis upon ball handling. To develop tactical awareness in a simple competitive game. To encourage pupils to organise and regulate their own activity.

†† *Individual warm-up; paired skill development; groups of 6 for game.*

⏱ *Warm-up 3–4 minutes; skill development 10–15 minutes; game 15 minutes.*

Previous skills/knowledge needed

The children need the ability to throw and catch consistently with a partner, when stationary and when on the move; and to work co-operatively with a partner. They should appreciate the need for rules in a competitive game.

Key background information

The ability of children halfway through Key Stage 2 to make sense of visual information relating to space and movement around them, together with better-established techniques in basic throwing and catching, enables them to exercise more complicated and rapid decision-making. They are now able to conceptualise strategies and tactics, and to see the need for planning in order to outwit an opponent. Because these abilities are at a relatively early stage of development, competitive games situations should be kept relatively simple; games should be conditioned to favour the team in possession of the ball, for instance four 'attackers' versus two 'defenders'.

The following teaching points will be useful:

▲ *Keeping possession of the ball is very important – try not to pass unless you are certain that your pass will reach its destination.*

▲ *Do not pass until the receiver is ready and aware.*

▲ *If you think you are in a good position to receive the ball, hold out your hands as a target for your team-mate.*

▲ *Try to get as far away from your opponents as possible before accepting a pass.*

Preparation

Make the appropriate warm-up activity cards (laminated, if possible) from sheet 110 to distribute to the class.

Resources needed

One large ball between two, defined working areas (ideally a grid consisting of a number of 10-metre squares on the playground or field, as shown in Figure 1), coloured bands or bibs, activity cards copied from photocopiable sheet 110.

Figure 1

←10m→
10m

What to do

Warm-up activity

Choose an individual warm-up activity from photocopiable sheet 110 and ask the children to practise it for 3–4 minutes.

Skill development

Organise the children into pairs; make sure each pair has a large ball, and ask them to practise the following activities:

▲ *Stand 5 metres (strides) apart and pass the ball to your partner with two hands. How many passes can you make in 20 seconds?*

▲ *Now try the same activity on the move. Keep a careful watch out for others: don't pass if there is anyone in the way.*

▲ *Now combine your pair with another pair making a four. Practise the same activity (passing on the move) making sure that everybody in your group passes and receives the ball an equal number of times in 5 minutes. Make sure that you remain within the working area.*

Game activity

Now progress to a competitive game of 4 versus 2. Organise the children into groups of 6. Ask them to nominate two 'chasers', who put on a coloured band or bib. The objective is to see how many successful passes the group of 4 can make in a given time without the ball being dropped, intercepted by one of the 'chasers' or passed outside the game area. When the ball is caught, no movement is allowed. Restrict each group to a 10 metre square working area and make sure that the 'chasers' are alternated frequently.

The above activities should be modified in future lessons to include kicking skills and work with a hockey stick.

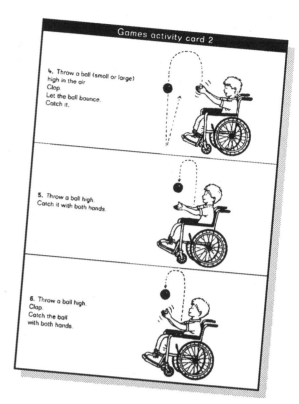

Directional play with combined passing towards a goal, line, or skittle may be introduced, but keep the defenders in the minority (for example, 3 versus 1 or 4 versus 2).

The same game can be played by passing and receiving with feet or with a hockey stick. Players will have to stop the ball, or else pass it straight on, without travelling with it.

Suggestion(s) for extension

Some more able children may be able to play with equal sides, but no more than 3 versus 3.

An element of travelling – moving with the ball – may gradually be introduced, but no more than two steps initially.

Suggestion(s) for support

For children having difficulty, delay the competitive element until receiving on the move and passing become better-established. Continue to set targets: *How many passes can you make in two minutes without dropping the ball?*

Assessment opportunities

Observe particularly the way in which the children make decisions about when and where to pass: do they properly assess the situation before they pass, or do they rush things and make errors too frequently?

Is the passing and catching technique of the children consistent, and does it hold up under competition? Is it sufficiently well-developed to free some of their attention for the observation of team-mates and opponents?

Reference to photocopiable sheet

Photocopiable sheet 110 shows three introductory activities, any one of which can be given to the children (as a card) to prompt their 'warm-up' activity.

PHYSICAL EDUCATION

INVASION GAMES –
Y5 & Y6 (P6 & P7)

To consolidate ball-handling and passing skills in the context of a fast-moving, small-side ball game. To develop knowledge of attacking and defensive strategies commonly used in invasion games.

†† *Individual warm-up; groups of 6 for skill development; groups of 6 or 8 for game.*

🕐 *Warm-up activity 5 minutes; skill development 10–15 minutes; game 15 minutes.*

Previous skills/knowledge needed
The children should be able to send and receive a pass on the move; and to make informed decisions about passing opportunities within a competitive game, particularly in terms of finding free space away from opponents.

Key background information
Sensory development (for example, a faster reaction time) allied to cumulative experience enables pupils at the end of Key Stage 2 to make sense of time and space in the context of a relatively fast-moving competitive game. Nevertheless, the vast majority of pupils will still need to remain within small-side versions of traditional games. This will encourage maximum learning through constant involvement in the game and frequent exposure to its skill requirements. Heavy emphasis on specialised positional play should be avoided at this stage; all children should experience attacking and defensive roles in free-flowing mini-games where possible.

The following teaching points will be useful:
▲ *Try to put as much distance as possible between yourself and your opponents before receiving a pass.*
▲ *When you are attacking, space in which to receive a pass can usually be found towards the touch-lines. Use it!*
▲ *Always try to move on after giving a pass.*
▲ *When defending, make sure you position yourself between your opponent and the goal or line that he/she is attacking.*

Preparation
Prepare the appropriate warm-up activity cards (laminated, if possible) from sheet 112 to distribute to the class.

Resources needed
One large ball per pupil, coloured games bibs, games posts or skittles; several marked playing areas of approximately tennis-court size in the playground or on the field; activity cards copied from photocopiable sheet 112.

What to do
Warm-up activity
Choose an individual warm-up activity from sheet 112, to be practised for two to three minutes by the whole class.

Skill development
Organise the class into groups of six and ask them to form a circle about six or seven metres in diameter to practise **'pass and follow'**. Pupils can pass the ball anywhere in the circle, but must immediately follow the pass to take up the position of the receiver. The receiver immediately passes the ball and moves on in the same way. The activity continues for two to three minutes. (See Figure 2.)

Game activity
Organise the class into groups of six or eight, and allocate them to a playing area to play 3 versus 3 or 4 versus 4. The objective could be to knock your opponents' skittle over with the ball; to bounce the ball in your opponents' hoop; or simply to make a pass to a team-mate over your opponents' goal line. Whatever the point-scoring element of the game is, the ball has to be passed by the team in possession successfully down the pitch in the direction of the opponents' 'goal'. Give the children opportunities to develop and consolidate the rules as play progresses by asking such questions as:
▲ *How does the other team get the ball?*
▲ *What happens when the ball goes out of play?*
▲ *Are you allowed to move with the ball? When?*
▲ *How do you restart play after a goal has been scored?*
Remember to reinforce the attacking and defensive principles referred to in the teaching points above.

Suggestion(s) for extension
If children require greater challenge in the skill development phase of the lesson, organise them into threes to practise 'square passing'. Make some six-metre squares with skittles (or use existing lines). The children must position themselves at three corners of their squares, leaving one corner vacant.

PHYSICAL
EDUCATION

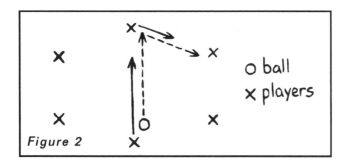

Figure 2

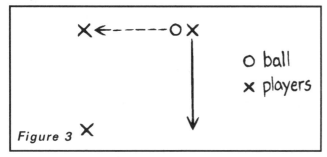

Figure 3

The ball must always be passed in the same direction around the square, with the sender running in the *opposite* direction to the pass. This activity will help the children to make decisions about precisely when to pass and when to delay. (See Figure 3.)

Suggestion(s) for support

For those children experiencing difficulty with the game activity, revert to 4 attackers versus 2 defenders. This will give the team in possession of the ball more time and freedom to plan and execute their attacking moves.

Assessment opportunities

Look out for the ways in which children are able to outflank the defence by accurately passing the ball to team-mates who are taking up positions at the edge of the playing area. How well do the children generally free themselves from opponents; do they use the full width of the playing area to do this? How often do defenders allow themselves to be drawn out of position, leaving their 'goal' vulnerable to attack?

Look out for children's ability to regulate their own games, devising additional or alternative rules if necessary.

Reference to photocopiable sheet

Sheet 112 shows three ball control and/or passing exercises, one of which can be copied as an activity card and given to the children to prompt their 'warm-up' exercise.

STRIKING/FIELDING GAMES – Y3 & Y4 (P4 AND P5)

To develop basic striking, fielding and throwing skills using a soft ball.

†† *Individual warm-up activity; paired skill development; game in groups of six.*

⏱ *Warm-up activity 5 minutes; skill development 10–15 minutes; game 15 minutes.*

Previous skills/knowledge needed

The children need the ability to catch a ball thrown by a partner from a short distance with reasonable consistency; to strike a thrown ball with a large round bat; and to work co-operatively with a partner and within a small group.

Key background information

Children at the beginning of Key Stage 2 are rapidly developing their hand-eye co-ordination. Catching and striking a ball with confidence is within the capability of most children providing the ball is not thrown by their partner too quickly or unpredictably. Activities involving some competition will provide an appropriate challenge for the majority; but consolidation of technique, with lots of opportunities for individual practice, should provide the main focus.

The following key teaching points will be useful:
▲ *Make sure your feet are well-spaced when throwing, catching and striking – you need to be well-balanced.*
▲ *Watch the ball all the way into your hands when catching and onto your bat when striking.*
▲ *Always try to use both hands when catching.*
▲ *Before starting your throw, take the ball as far back with your hand as you can.*
▲ *When batting, grip your bat firmly but try to keep your wrist(s) loose.* **Use both hands** *to hold the bat whenever you find this to be more effective or comfortable.*

PHYSICAL
EDUCATION

Preparation

If practical, enlarge a selection of activity cards from photocopiable sheets 110, 111 and 112 and display them around the working area.

Resources needed

One small/medium-sized soft ball for each child, one large round wooden or plastic bat for each child, activity cards copied from photocopiable sheets (see above).

What to do

Warm-up activity

Choose an activity card from sheets 110, 111 and 112. Ask the class to practise this activity individually for five minutes.

Skill development

Organise the class into pairs, with one ball between two. They stand five strides apart. One partner rolls the ball to the other, who fields it (remembering to stand fully behind the ball and bend his/her knees to collect it) and then returns the ball with an underhand throw to the first partner. They repeat this activity 10 times and then change roles.

Next, they repeat the activity, but roll the ball to either side of their partners, so that the fielders have to move to

collect the ball before returning it with a throw. Make sure that the children have plenty of space for this activity.

Now one partner collects a bat. The other partner throws the ball gently from five strides to the batter, who hits the ball for the other to catch. After 10 hits, they change over. Now ask the children to count how many hits and catches they can make in three minutes. This task requires that the bowler throws accurately and the batter hits with control.

Game activity

Organise the class into groups of six: one batter, one bowler and 4 fielders. To each group, allocate a working space to play **'Beat the fielders'**. The objective of this game is for the batter to hit the ball past or over the fielders, so that it crosses a boundary line (see Figure 4). If the batter hits over the fielders and the boundary line, he/she gets two points; hitting past the fielders to the boundary line earns one point. Each batter has six attempts and then the children rotate positions. The batter accumulating the most points from six turns wins.

Suggestion(s) for extension

For those pupils requiring greater challenge with hand-eye co-ordination:

▲ Encourage them to throw overhand as well as underhand, stressing accuracy rather than speed of return.

▲ Increase the distance between bowler and batter.

Suggestion(s) for support

Equip children who are experiencing difficulty with a larger ball and bats with a broader striking surface, in order to increase the likelihood of making contact when batting.

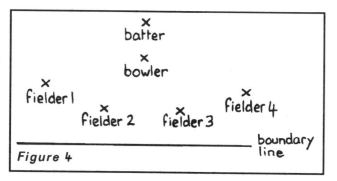

Figure 4

Games

Assessment opportunities

Observe the throwing, fielding and batting technique of the class. Are they able to throw accurately when bowling to a batter or returning the ball as a fielder? Are they able to judge the flight and path of a moving ball and make effective catches or stops? Do they make firm contact with the ball on a regular and consistent basis when batting?

Reference to photocopiable sheets

The activity cards on sheets 110, 111 and 112 can be copied and used to provide a range of warm-up activities.

STRIKING/FIELDING GAMES – Y4 & Y5 (P5 & P6)

To consolidate and further develop batting, throwing, catching and fielding skills. To introduce team activities associated with striking and fielding games.

†† *Individual warm-up; teams of about 8 players for skill development; teams of about 4 players for game.*

🕐 *Warm-up activity 5 minutes; skill development 15 minutes; batting and fielding game 15 minutes.*

Previous skills/knowledge needed

The children need the ability to catch and field a medium-paced soft ball with consistency and confidence; and to throw a soft ball accurately, underarm, over short distances. They need consistency in striking a soft ball with a round-faced wooden/plastic bat when the ball is thrown underarm.

Key background information

Pupils midway through Key Stage 2 should have developed their individual striking and fielding skills to the point where they can begin to apply their techniques to a competitive team game. Maximum involvement for all children is essential.

As much opportunity as possible should be provided to develop and refine techniques within a more demanding situation, where the efforts of team-mates and opponents have increasingly to be reckoned with.

The following teaching points will be useful:

▲ *When catching and fielding, watch the ball all the way into your hands.*

▲ *When fielding a moving ball, always try to get behind it.*

▲ *When you are throwing, a good follow-through with the arm will produce greater speed and distance.*

▲ *When batting, try to hit THROUGH the path of the ball rather than across it. Turning your body sideways-on to the path of the ball will help you achieve this.*

Preparation

Provide a selection of laminated activity cards from photocopiable sheet 113 to distribute around the class for warm-up and individual practice.

Resources needed

An ample supply of small soft balls, such as tennis balls (at least one per child), wooden or plastic round-faced bats, small wooden or plastic cricket bats, a large playing area with a good surface such as the playground, activity cards copied from photocopiable sheet 113.

What to do

Warm-up activity

Choose an appropriate activity from sheet 113 and ask the children to practise it individually for five minutes.

Skill development

Divide the class into two groups. It may be useful to do this in terms of their general ball-handling abilities. Allocate a defined playing area to each group (if there are approximately 16 pupils in each group, an area the size of a netball court would be appropriate) in order to play **Team Fielding**.

This game is best played in teams of about 8 players. (If there are more than 32 in the class, have more than four teams; if there are fewer than 32, have smaller teams.) The aim is to roll a tennis ball over your opponents' goal-line to a team-mate. Play commences on one team's goal-line, and the ball is 'passed' down the court by a team rolling it to their own players who are free of markers. The defenders must try to intercept the ball – when they do, they gain possession and become the attackers.

This game is a vigorous and enjoyable way of combining elements of fielding and invasion games. It is useful to ask the children to modify the game with some of their own rules, using questions such as: *How many points win the game? What happens if the ball is rolled outside the playing area? How long can you hold the ball before rolling it?*

Game activity
Conclude the lesson with a game of **Gate Rounders**. This game combines elements of rounders and cricket, but is played with small sides. It encourages the batters to hit through the ball rather than across it. Organise the children into teams of four players, and allocate each game of 4 versus 4 to a playing area. Points are scored in the following ways by the batting side: 1 point when the ball is hit; 2 points when a 'run' is scored; 3 points when the ball is hit through the 'gate'. A run is scored by the batter running to the bowler's end and back. A fielder cannot position him/herself between the batter and the 'gate'.

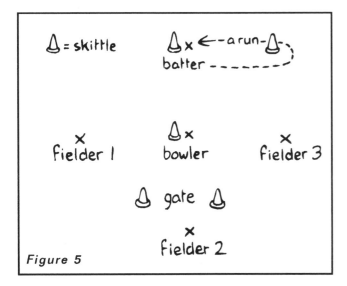

Figure 5

Set out the playing area as shown in Figure 5. Every player on the fielding side must bowl an 'over' of six balls. Every batter faces six balls, no matter how many times he/she is out. Batters may be either caught or run out. The only consequence of being out is that no points are scored off that particular ball. Batters are run out if they fail to get back to the batting base before the ball is returned to the bowler.

Batters may try to take more than one run off a particular hit. The winning team is the one that scores the most points off 24 balls (or in a series of innings).

Suggestion(s) for extension
Children with good striking skills should be encouraged to use a cricket bat with both hands, rather than a round-faced bat. Equally, they might use a rounders bat with a one-handed action. (They should *not* be encouraged to use a cricket bat with one hand, since this can place a dangerous strain on the wrist.) When the ball is being returned from the outfield, overarm throwing should be encouraged.

Suggestion(s) for support
Children with poor striking skills will do better using a larger soft ball, This will make contact with the ball more frequent and predictable. The game will be played at a slower pace, and will present more appropriate challenges for children experiencing slower development in hand-eye co-ordination.

Assessment opportunities
Observe how confidently children strike the ball and how frequently they make firm contact with it. How well do children field a moving ball: do they stop it effectively, and are they able to return it accurately with a fluent action?

Reference to photocopiable sheet
The three activities shown on sheet 113 can be copied as activity cards for use in the children's warm-up exercises.

STRIKING/FIELDING GAMES – Y5 & Y6 (P6 & P7)

To introduce and develop small-side competitive team games encompassing major elements of traditional striking/fielding games. To consolidate throwing skills, with a particular emphasis upon accuracy.

**†† ** *Individual warm-up activity; skill development in pairs or two teams; game in four teams.*

🕐 *Warm-up activity 5 minutes; skill development 10 minutes; game 20 minutes.*

Previous skills/knowledge needed
The children need the ability to throw, catch and field a small ball with confidence; and to strike a small ball, using a variety of implements, with reasonable power.

Key background information
The majority of children towards the end of Key Stage 2 should be able to display the basic techniques of throwing, catching, fielding and striking in a confident manner. Regular individual practice will still be required to retain and consolidate efficient techniques; indeed, every games lesson ought to include an opportunity for children to work individually with a ball on selected aspects of skilled performance. Developmental gains (psychological and social as well as physical) will allow children aged 10 to 11 to free their attention increasingly from monitoring the effects of their own actions to devising strategies and plans in order to maximise their own team performance and outwit their opponents. Thus many pupils at this age are able to compete in team games in a meaningful and productive way.

Teachers should be aware of the following principles relating to striking/fielding games, with a view to developing effective decision-making in their pupils together with a better understanding of the use of appropriate tactics:

▲ When batting, players should observe where the fielders have chosen to position themselves and look for any gaps through which the ball might be hit.

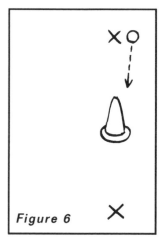

Figure 6

▲ *Fielders may set an* **attacking** *or a* **defensive** *field. An attacking field usually involves the fielders standing closer to the batters in the hope of catching them out. Such a field can be used to good effect when your team has batted first and has scored lots of points or runs. A defensive field involves spreading out the fielders, covering as much ground as possible in order to stop the batters scoring too freely.*

▲ *'Backing up' is an important feature of good fielding. Whenever return throws are made from the outfield to the bowler, for instance, or a batter strikes a ball towards a fielder, it is always wise to present a 'back-up': a second fielder moving into a position behind the first receiver, in case he/she misfields or misjudges the path of the ball.*

Preparation
Prepare a selection of appropriate activity cards from photocopiable sheets 112 and 113 to distribute among the class for the warm-up activity.

Resources needed
Tennis balls (one between two), cricket and rounders bats, skittles, rounders posts, free-standing wickets, a large playing area, sufficient for at least four mini-games of cricket or rounders, activity cards copied from sheets 112 and 113.

What to do
Warm-up activity
Choose an activity from the activity bank (see 'Preparation') and ask the class to practise it individually for 5 minutes.
Skill development
Organise the class into pairs, preferably of similar ball-skill ability. Organise the class as shown in Figure 6, with partners facing each other on either side of a 'target' skittle. The objective is to hit the skittle with accurate throwing; but the activity will also provide useful fielding practice for the partner facing the thrower. They should alternate throws. Let each pair decide initially how far away from the skittle they will stand. After sufficient practice, make the activity competitive by keeping the distance from the skittle the same for every pair and looking for the first pair to make, say, six 'hits'.

Game activities

Divide the class into two and line them up on opposite sides of a netball court, behind the touchlines. Equip each pupil with a tennis ball. The objective is to 'drive' a football over the opponents' goal line by striking it with the tennis balls, which must be thrown from behind the touchline. This activity will encourage good fielding as well as accurate throwing, since the sooner the throws of opponents are collected the more throws a team will be able to make. It is important that each team remains behind its respective touchline.

Then organise the class into four groups of similar overall ability and set up two mini-cricket and two mini-rounders games with teams of four players. If there are more than 32 players, have larger teams (up to six players) or more teams. Make sure that each game has sufficient space. Follow the procedures outlined in the previous lesson (see page 32), making sure that all the children get the same amount of time batting, bowling and fielding. In other respects, the rules and methods of scoring can replicate the full game. It may help with skill development to make sure that at least four successive weeks are spent by the same groups on either rounders or cricket, before changing them over.

Suggestion(s) for extension

More confident children should be given the opportunity to work with a hard ball. The hard plastic variety which comes with Kwik-Cricket is particularly suitable and safe for both rounders and cricket. In mini-cricket, overarm bowling should be encouraged wherever possible and the length of the pitch adjusted where necessary to accommodate this.

Suggestion(s) for support

Allow less confident children to play with a larger, soft ball and a large enough bat to ensure consistent success in striking the ball. With some children, it may be necessary to dispense with the bat and allow them to strike with one hand.

Assessment opportunities

Observe how well the children organise themselves when fielding. Do they respond to the strengths of the batter? Do they remain alert and back up each other's fielding? Do they strike the ball consistently well when batting and exploit weaknesses in the field? Can they organise their own play, keeping scores accurately and observing agreed rules?

Reference to photocopiable sheets

Photocopiable sheets 112 and 113 show basic ball control exercises which can be used as warm-up activities.

OVER THE NET GAMES – Y4 & Y5 (P5 & P6)

To develop basic techniques associated with striking a ball over a barrier (the 'net'). To develop an understanding of continuity in net games ('the rally').
†† *Individual warm-up activity; paired skill development and game activity.*
🕐 *Warm-up activity 5 minutes; skill development and game 30 minutes.*

Previous skills/knowledge needed

The children need to be able to play individually, striking a soft ball against a wall with control using an open palm or a wooden/plastic bat, and sustaining the activity by hitting the ball on the volley or after one bounce.

Key background information

Throughout KS1 and the beginning of KS2, pupils should have been given frequent opportunities to develop and consolidate their striking skills through individual practice and in a variety of simple game situations. From the middle of KS2, many children will be able to apply their basic striking action to the disciplined challenge of having to hit the ball quickly into a fairly small area on the other side of a net.

The following teaching points will be useful:
▲ *When striking the ball make sure you are well balanced with your feet spaced out. Stay on your toes!*
▲ *Always try to get sideways-on to the ball, so that you can hit the ball horizontally and straight.*
▲ *Try to keep your racket/bat high. This will save you time in preparing to hit the ball.*
▲ *Watch where your opponent is standing and try to hit the ball away from him/her when playing competitively.*

Preparation

Prepare a selection of activity cards from photocopiable sheet 113, to distribute among the class for their warm-up activity.

Resources needed

One ball and one bat/racket per child (vinyl-covered foam balls of large tennis-ball size, with their slow bounce properties, are particularly suitable); skittles and long canes to make 'nets'; skipping ropes to make court markings; activity cards copied from photocopiable sheet 113.

What to do

Warm-up activity

Ask the children to choose an activity from those on sheet 113 and practise it individually for five minutes.

Skill development

Organise the children into pairs, with a small light ball (see 'Resources needed') between two and a bat/racket each. Ask them to stand a short distance (five strides) apart and play the ball back and forth to each other continuously after one bounce. How long can they keep the 'rally' going? Remember to ask the children to stand sideways-on to the ball. When the children become confident, close the gap to three strides and ask them to play the ball to each other without a bounce (volleying). How many volleys can they make to each other before the ball touches the ground?

Game activity

Ask the children to set up 'courts'. They should use canes and skittles to improvise nets, and skipping ropes to make temporary court markings. Only the back line needs to be marked; it should initially be about five strides from the 'net', but can be increased if the players experience difficulty.

Each pair should play the ball continuously back and forth, making sure that it bounces either once within the marked

court area or not at all before being returned over the 'net'. How long can the pair maintain a rally? Can they make up a game using this activity as a basis or starting point?

Suggestion(s) for extension

Children with well-developed striking skills and good hand-eye co-ordination should be encouraged to use both 'forehand' and 'backhand' strokes, according to the path of the ball relative to their position.

Suggestion(s) for support

For children who are less confident in their striking skills, it may be helpful to introduce the 'net' but delay the extra challenge of a court marking – simply encourage the children to hit the ball consistently to their partner over the barrier, perhaps allowing more than one bounce before returning it.

Assessment opportunities

Observe how well the children can sustain a co-operative rally. Can they strike the ball so that it consistently lands in the opposite court? Are they prepared to move towards the ball in order to make an effective return?

Reference to photocopiable sheet

The three activities on sheet 113 can be copied as activity cards for use in the children's warm-up exercise.

OVER THE NET GAMES – Y5 & Y6 (P6 & P7)

To consolidate striking skills over a net. To introduce competitive court play and develop an understanding of basic court tactics and strategies.

†† *Individual warm-up activity; paired skill development and game activities.*

⏱ *Warm-up activity 5 minutes; skill development 15 minutes; game activity 15 minutes.*

Previous skills/knowledge needed

The children need the ability to strike a small soft ball with control and accuracy using playbats and/or plastic rackets; and to judge the flight of a moving ball and move quickly towards it in order to make a return.

Key background information

Children at the end of the key stage have developed and refined their striking skills through individual practice and work with a partner. Much of this work (particularly in 'over the net' games) will necessarily have been undertaken co-operatively, as in sustaining a rally. However, the competitive versions of such games involve outplaying an opponent – usually by returning the ball as far away as possible from

where he/she is positioned. Thus the teacher may be required at this point to alter children's habits which have become established in the process of building up basic techniques.

The following teaching points will be useful:

▲ *A position close to the net will create more attacking opportunities and allow you to hit the ball away from your opponent; alternatively, a position back from the net will allow greater coverage of your court and make for better defence.*
▲ *Try to avoid playing the ball into the middle of your opponent's court, where it will be easy to return; play the ball deep into your opponent's court, or short, or at an angle – anywhere that makes your opponent run to retrieve it!*
▲ *Stay on your toes and keep your racket/bat high!*

Preparation
Prepare a selection of activity cards from photocopiable sheet 113 to distribute among the class for their warm-up activity.

Resources needed
Skittles, cones, skipping ropes, tennis balls or foam rubber balls, playbats (wood or light plastic).

What to do
Warm-up activity
Let the children choose an activity from photocopiable sheet 113 and practise it individually for five minutes.
Skill development
Organise the class into pairs and allocate each pair to a 'singles court' improvised with skittles and canes or skipping ropes (or use a 10m by 10m square in a pre-marked coaching grid). Ask the children to practise freely in their pairs, with both partners initially positioned at the back of the court and hitting the ball deep. After five minutes, they should move closer to the 'net' to practise close volleying.
Game activity
Now let each pair play competitively. They should devise ways of scoring and starting their games – for example, starting with an improvised 'service'.

Suggestion(s) for extension
Some children will find playing a doubles version of the game challenges them further. Not only have they to be aware of their opponents, they also must work successfully with their partner in attack and (particularly) defence.

Suggestion(s) for support
Some children may still be experiencing difficulty with striking. Learning to use the court effectively depends on experiencing continuous play and being able to sustain a rally. Thus, in order to give children who have not yet mastered basic striking technique (and have already tried using bigger bats and balls) an experience of court play, encourage them to play the game by throwing the ball (a large foam ball is particularly effective) over the net with two hands.

Assessment opportunities
Observe how well the children are able to regulate their own activity. Are they able to keep score responsibly and apply the rules consistently? Are they able to sustain the game, or does it break down frequently? Do they use the court effectively and make their opponents run about?

Reference to photocopiable sheet
The three activities on sheet 113 can be copied as activity cards for use in the children's warm-up exercise.

POTTED SPORTS

To reinforce a range of basic ball skills: dribbling, passing and striking. To develop team and social skills in a competitive game situation. To exercise responsibility though devising an agreed scoring system and keeping score reliably.

†† *Individual warm-up activity; groups of six for games.*

🕓 *Warm-up 5 minutes; game activities 45 minutes.*

Previous skills/knowledge needed
The children need to be able to work in teams. They need to have confidence and consistency in a range of basic ball skills involving: close control of a ball with feet, hands and hockey stick; striking a ball; and aiming and receiving a ball.

Key background information
This activity will provide a useful opportunity for children to develop a number of basic ball skills under the pressure of needing to perform these skills as quickly as possible. The teacher will need to keep a careful eye on the children's techniques and make sure that actions are not hurried and rushed (which would bring its own penalties, since to lose control of the ball will automatically cost time).

When all teams have completed the five activities, ask each team leader to add up their total number of points and see which is the winning team.

Suggestion(s) for extension
The activities could be made more difficult by: reducing the space between skittles; asking the children to use their weaker foot or hand when involved in a dribbling activity; or allowing only volleying returns (not allowing the ball to bounce) in the over-the-net activity.

Suggestion(s) for support
This activity is about team competition; in order to keep the competition fair, it may not be practical to modify the activities on an individual basis. It thus remains essential that all teams recognise and value the efforts of each team member.

Assessment opportunities
The teacher should observe how well the children perform in each activity, and whether they are able to demonstrate sound techniques when required to work quickly. Equally important, it will be possible to judge how effectively the children work together in a team.

Reference to photocopiable sheet
Photocopiable sheet 114 is a task sheet setting certain parameters for five game activities; the children have to decide on the full set of rules for playing. The sheet can also be used to record a group's results.

Preparation
Provide one copy per team of photocopiable sheet 114.

Resources needed
Hockey sticks, skittles, hard balls (large and small), canes, hoops, recording sheets (photocopiable sheet 114 can easily be used for this), a whistle, a stop-watch. The partner activities will require enough equipment for each group to keep three pairs going at the same time.

What to do
After a warm-up activity, organise the class into groups of six. Try to create an even mix of boys and girls, as well as of ability. Let the children decide the scoring system for each activity – in activity A, the obvious way of scoring would be to award one point every time the ball is struck accurately between the skittles to a partner who returns it in the same way. Point out to the children that if they decide to place the skittles too far apart and stand close to them they may score too many points in five minutes to keep count! Similarly, in activity B, the children can make their own decisions about how far apart the skittles should be placed and whether a point should be gained every time a player passes a skittle, or only when the whole course has been negotiated. Encourage the children to devise difficult but realistic challenges. Once the activity 'rules' have been agreed, they must remain the same for every team.

Remember that this is a competition against the clock: each group has to accumulate as many points as possible in each activity (which can be timed by the teacher, though this task could provide meaningful involvement for a non-participant). A whistle should be used to signal the start and finish of each five-minute period. Allow the children at least two minutes between activities for recording and recovery.

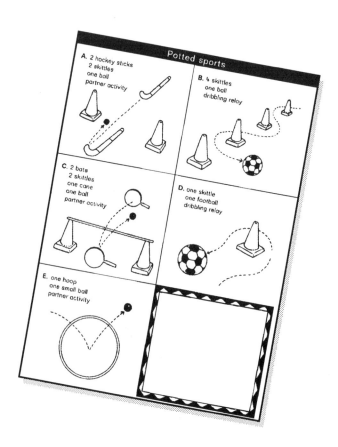

PHYSICAL EDUCATION

Gymnastics

Of all the activities taught within the National Curriculum for Physical Education, perhaps Gymnastics offers to pupils the best insight into the workings, possibilities and limitations of their bodies in movement. Gymnastics is concerned with acquiring control, co-ordination and versatility in using the body and responding to challenges. It also helps children to understand their own physiology, particularly the components of strength, suppleness and (to a lesser degree) stamina. In addition, gymnastics promotes spatial awareness and decision-making.

Work in gymnastics focuses essentially on **what** the body can do. These are sometimes called the **Basic Actions**: travelling, turning, rolling, jumping, balancing, swinging and climbing. In the primary school, these actions need to be explored, refined and combined in order to provide **variety in movement**. They can be varied in terms of **where** they are performed (different levels, pathways, directions, on the floor, on/against/over apparatus, opposite/alongside a partner) and **how** they are performed (different speeds, different body shapes). The final goal in gymnastics is to combine a series of actions into a fluent movement sequence.

Effective lessons in gymnastics are characterised by: good class organisation; high levels of pupil activity and involvement; a safe, yet challenging, teaching and learning environment; a brisk pace, but with opportunities for consolidation and reflection; movement tasks which reflect the capabilities and needs of the children.

PHYSICAL
EDUCATION

The gymnastics lesson

This chapter contains a number of sample gymnastics lessons which suggest the kind of work which might be appropriate at certain points in Key Stage 2. Three lessons illustrate work for early in the key stage (Y3/P4); three lessons are appropriate to mid-key stage work (Y4 and Y5/ P5 and P6); and three lessons serve to illustrate work at the end of the key stage (Y6/P7). The sequence of lessons within each phase is progressive. The lesson plans themselves are supplemented with a range of photocopiable resource materials including skill development cards, partner work cards and sequence building cards. (The skill development cards are intended to remind **teachers** of the key points and progressions in various gymnastic actions. Remember not to give children too many teaching points to think about at one time.) A 'warm-up activity bank' is also included as a photocopiable sheet, from which teachers can select two or three activities to commence each gymnastics lesson.

It should be emphasised that the suggested duration for each lesson should not be interpreted too literally. The material included in any one lesson plan may well represent a much more extended unit of work for many children. Progress through the lesson material ultimately depends upon the responses that the children make: the teacher should be satisfied that **both quality and variety of movement** have been achieved before moving on to a new theme or task.

It should be emphasised here that gymnastics involves much more than performance. At the end of their primary education, the gymnastics curriculum should have equipped pupils:

▲ to develop further the variety and quality of performance of the basic actions;

▲ to combine basic actions and to develop the ability to move smoothly from one action to another;

▲ to explore, select, practice and refine longer and more complex sequences, involving a wide range of skills, on the floor and on apparatus;

▲ to appreciate the need to follow instructions, rules and routines;

▲ to lift, carry and place apparatus safely, with an increasing degree of independence;

▲ to work effectively with a partner when developing sequences;

▲ to describe and understand the short-term effects of exercise on the body;

▲ to appreciate the need for practice when seeking improvement in skilled performance, and to develop a willingness to persevere and to make the best effort possible;

▲ to appreciate that **thought** is critical to successful performance;

▲ to share ideas and listen to one another, and to appreciate the contributions made by other class members;

▲ to describe, compare and contrast movements, to reflect upon the merits of their performance and that of their peers, and to suggest ways of improving;

▲ to apply feedback and guidance from the teacher to improve individual skills and relate new skills to those already mastered;

▲ to understand the possibilities and limitations of the body when attempting movement tasks;

▲ to experience success and enjoyment and to develop self-confidence.

Safety in gymnastics

Successful teaching in gymnastics ensures that the children are given appropriate physical challenges. It is critical, however, that all reasonable precautions and safety procedures are observed by the teacher in order to maintain safe working practice in what is a potentially hazardous environment. Several features characterise safe practice in gymnastics.

▲ **A positive classroom atmosphere.** Remember that gymnastics is for all children, irrespective of their ability. Children feel secure and happy in their work when the tasks and expectations are realistic and clearly understood, and when co-operation is valued.

▲ **Firm discipline.** This is essential at all times. It is of critical importance that the children are taught to respond immediately to commands such as 'Stop!'; 'Stop and sit!'; 'Stop, climb down from your apparatus'.

▲ **Pupils must display a sound knowledge of the following:**

• Entry and exit from the hall or gymnasium. The children should know exactly where to go and what to do on entering the hall. They should always leave the hall in a quiet and orderly manner.

• Appropriate noise levels. There should be an expectation that the children work silently and with full concentration. In partner work situations, children should communicate with each other as quietly as possible.

• Lesson structure. Lessons begin with a warm-up activity; then progress to floor work, followed by apparatus work; then conclude with a cool-down activity.

• Apparatus handling. The class will need to know how many children are needed to carry a given item of equipment, and to demonstrate safe lifting technique when moving benches, mats, boxes and so on.

Gymnastics Key Stage progression

Throughout Key Stage 2, the children should adapt, refine and practise, both on the floor and on apparatus, the basic actions of:

▲ rolling;
▲ turning;
▲ swinging;
▲ jumping;
▲ climbing;
▲ balancing;
▲ travelling on hands and feet.

The actions should place the emphasis on changes of:

▲ speed;
▲ level;
▲ body shape;
▲ pathway;
▲ direction.

The children should have the opportunity to make more complex and repeatable movement sequences in response to set tasks.

In every year group, the theme of **travelling** will provide the basis of the work. Travelling falls into three main categories:

1. Travelling using feet, for example jumping, walking, hopping, running, skipping.
2. Travelling using hands and feet, for example bunny jumps, cartwheels.
3. Travelling using different body parts, for example rolling, sliding.

The children should learn the five **basic jumps** which are compatible with travelling on the feet:

1. Take off on one foot, land on both feet.
2. Take off on one foot, land on same foot.
3. Take off on one foot, land on other foot.
4. Take off on both feet, land on one foot.
5. Take off on both feet, land on both feet.

Year 3 (P4)

Main focus of the work: making sequences by linking different actions (floor, small apparatus and large apparatus) around the theme of travelling.

▲ Pupils will need to understand that a sequence has a beginning, middle and end and that linking different actions needs to be done smoothly.

Year 4 (P5)

Main focus of the work: development of the five basic jumps around the themes of flight and travelling.

▲ Pupils will need to know what makes for a safe and resilient landing.

▲ They should be introduced to body shapes involving symmetry and asymmetry, and to partner work (copying and following, using the floor and mats).

▲ They should be reminded about the need to concentrate on the quality of performance and to make clear, definite body shapes.

▲ They should be given opportunities to judge how well they and others co-operate in partner work tasks.

Year 5 (P6)

Main focus: partner work around the themes of travelling and transference of body weight.

▲ Pupils should be introduced to partner work involving matching and mirroring, using apparatus.

▲ They should be reminded about the need for good extension in movement.

▲ They should be required to make simple comments and judgements about their own performance and that of others.

Year 6 (P7)

Main focus: further development of partner work around the themes of travelling, balance and flight.

▲ Pupils will need to be introduced to counterbalance with a partner and using a partner as an obstacle.

▲ They will need to refine complex individual sequences demonstrating good control for display purposes, showing contrasts in shape, speed and direction.

▲ They will need to make simple comments and judgements about their own performance and that of others.

Y3 (P4) – LESSON 1

To develop selected individual actions around the theme of travelling without using the feet.

†† *Individual warm-up; individual and paired gymnastic activity; individual conclusion.*

🕐 *Warm-up activity 2 minutes; gymnastic activity 30 minutes; conclusion 2 minutes.*

Previous skills/knowledge needed

The children should have previous experience of basic rolling and balancing on the floor.

Key background information

The emphasis in this lesson should be placed upon quality of movement. The teacher will need to remind pupils about curling tightly, retaining a shape and then stretching out fully. It is also worth stressing from the outset that children should start and finish the movement with poise.

Preparation

The teacher will need photocopiable sheets 115 and 116, giving instructions for the pin roll, the dish roll, the egg roll and the shoulder stand. The warm-up activity bank (photocopiable sheet 117) will also be needed.

Resources needed

Gymnastic mats (one per pair of children), photocopiable sheets 115, 116 and 117.

What to do

Warm-up activity

Ask the children to enter the hall as quietly as possible and sit in a space. When the class is settled, commence the warm-up. Choose a warm-up activity from photocopiable sheet 117. The choice of warm-up activity will depend on the content of the lesson and the prevailing mood of the children. For example, if the children need livening up, then choose an activity such as running, jumping and stretching high. If they need settling down, then choose an activity such as running on the spot, curling and stretching.

Gymnastic activity

Ask the children to find their own space. Introduce the pin roll, using photocopiable sheet 115 to reinforce good technique. Allow enough time for practice. Ask children to demonstrate where appropriate, focusing on one teaching point at a time. Then move on to the egg roll (see photocopiable sheet 116) and repeat the process.

Then organise the children into pairs and ask them to set out their mats in a space. Tell/remind them about the rules of good lifting and careful placing:
▲ back straight, head up;
▲ fingers underneath the mat, thumbs on top of it;
▲ move slowly and look where you are going.

Ask the children to practise the dish roll (see photocopiable sheet 115), with one child in each pair working while the other observes and comments; then they change round. Help the children to improve their performance, using the photocopiable sheet.

Now ask the pairs of children to choose a balance using a large base (such as the back or shoulders) and hold it for at least 3 seconds, with one child on the mat and the other on the floor. Then they should change over.

Working one at a time while the other partner observes and comments (as above), they should practise the shoulder stand (see photocopiable sheet 116).

PHYSICAL EDUCATION

Conclusion

Now put the mats away and conclude the lesson with 'touch and travel'. Each child makes a curled shape in a space. When they are touched by the teacher, they must travel towards the door using their feet as little as possible, forming a queue for exit.

Suggestion(s) for extension

Ask the children to find a variety of ways of returning to their feet from the shoulder stand position.

Suggestion(s) for support

For those children who are less confident in maintaining a fully extended shoulder stand, ask them to make an 'L' shape with their upper body and legs. (See Figure 1.)

Assessment opportunities

Observe how well the children control their movement. Are they able to perform the movements slowly, with control? Are they able to maintain their body shape for the duration of the action? Do they make clearly defined starts and finishes.

Figure 1

Reference to photocopiable sheets

Photocopiable sheets 115 and 116 give instructions for four basic floor/mat actions which the teacher should explain to the children. (These sheets are for teacher use only, as a source of technical support.) Photocopiable sheet 117 provides a range of possible warm-up exercises, of which the teacher should select one as appropriate.

Y3 (P4) – LESSON 2

To develop sequence making by linking 'unlike' actions: balances and rolls. To perform the Arabesque. To describe, compare and contrast other children's performances.

†† *Individual warm-up; individual and paired gymnastic activity; individual conclusion.*

🕐 *Warm-up 2 minutes; gymnastic activity 30 minutes; conclusion 3 minutes.*

Previous skills/knowledge needed

The children should have experience of linking at least two 'like' actions. They will also need to understand the concept of balance (in this context: stillness in body shape).

Key background information

Teachers should be aware that there will always be variation in the quality of performance whenever children are set movement tasks. Some children will be able to achieve a 'T' shape in the Arabesque (see photocopiable sheet 118), whereas others will not be able to achieve such clarity in their body shape. Try to emphasise to all the children that extension of arms, legs and torso is important.

A movement sequence consists of a series of actions put together smoothly. The separate actions might be likened to the words of a sentence, which are put in the correct order to create something meaningful.

Preparation

The teacher will need to refer to the skill development card for the 'Arabesque' (photocopiable sheet 118); the 'Activities to encourage extension' card (photocopiable sheet 119); and the sequence development cards on photocopiable sheets 120 and 121. The teacher will also need to photocopy and cut out approximately six copies of each sequence strip (photocopiable sheets 120 and 121) for the children to use. Photocopiable sheet 122 could also be used as an extension activity.

Resources needed

Gymnastic mats (one per pair of children), photocopiable sheets 118 to 121, photocopiable sheet 122 (for extension activity only).

What to do
Warm-up activity

Ask the children to enter the hall as quietly as possible and sit in a space. When the class is settled, commence the warm-up. The choice of warm-up activity should depend on the content of the lesson. Photocopiable sheet 119 ('Activities to encourage extension') may be appropriate. The prevailing mood of the children will also help to determine what type of warm-up activity is appropriate (see page 42).

PHYSICAL
EDUCATION

Gymnastic activity

Now ask the children to find their own space. Can they show three different balances on their feet? After a few minutes' practice, introduce the Arabesque as a class activity. Use photocopiable sheet 118 to assist your technical guidance.

Divide the class into pairs. Try to pair more confident children with less confident ones. Then distribute the sequence building cards, one card to each child in a pair. For some children, sequence card 1 will represent an appropriate challenge. More confident children should be given sequence card 2. The three sequences given on each photocopiable sheet are identical, and will save the teacher time when photocopying for distribution to the children. Children should perform the sequence from left to right. These sequences are basic, and do not require additional linking movements – **fluency** is the quality to be emphasised here.

Allow plenty of time for practice; then select examples of fluent, controlled sequences to share with the class. Ask

the children to observe these sequences carefully and then describe what they see (with your help). Are the sequences put together smoothly? Do they contain three actions?

Conclusion

Ask the children to perform three different jumps on the floor (either from a standing start or with a short approach), concentrating on height and controlled landings. Look for stillness on landing. The children should land on the balls of their feet, with their knees bent (no more than 90°).

Suggestion(s) for extension

For those children displaying high levels of confidence, use the third sequence card (photocopiable sheet 122).

Suggestion(s) for support

For children who are less confident with reading, the teacher will need to provide abundant verbal and visual guidance to help them interpret the sequence cards. If the three-action sequence is too difficult for some children, a two-action sequence may be more appropriate.

Assessment opportunities

Observe how well the children demonstrate stillness and extension in the Arabesque position. Are they able to construct fluent three-action sequences using the sequence cards? Do they land with good control when jumping?

Reference to photocopiable sheets

Photocopiable sheet 118 can be used (by the teacher) to teach the 'Arabesque' balance. Sheet 119 shows a number of activities to develop physical extension; the teacher can select one of these as a warm-up activity. Sheets 120 and 121 each contain three identical sequence cards; these sheets can be photocopied (onto card), cut up into strips and distributed to the children as appropriate. The sequence cards on sheet 122 could be used as an extension.

PHYSICAL EDUCATION

Y3 (P4) – LESSON 3

To develop sequence building further, using benches and mats. To consolidate apparatus handling skills.

†† *Individual warm-up; gymnastic activity in apparatus groups; individual conclusion.*

⏲ *Warm-up 2 minutes; gymnastic activity 30 minutes; conclusion 2 minutes.*

Previous skills/knowledge needed

The children need to understand the concept of sequence building – that is, be able to say what a movement sequence is. They need to be able to work co-operatively and responsibly within an apparatus group.

Key background information

The children should be reminded that movement sequences have a beginning and end, and that the actions in the sequence need to be linked together smoothly.

Preparation

The teacher will need to ensure that the apparatus to be used is easily accessible. This is usually best achieved by dispersing the apparatus around the edge of the hall. To maximise the use of the available time, ask the children to describe what they achieved in the previous week's lesson while they are getting changed. The teacher will need a copy of photocopiable sheet 117.

Resources needed

Gymnastic mats, hoops, ropes and benches, photocopiable sheet 117.

What to do

Warm-up activity

Ask the children to enter the hall as quietly as possible and sit in a space. When the class is settled, commence the warm-up. Choose a suitable activity from the warm-up bank (photocopiable sheet 117). The choice of warm-up activity will depend on the content of the lesson and the prevailing mood of the children (see page 42).

Gymnastic activity

Ask the children to find a space and practise a previously learned movement sequence (see page 44). After a suitable amount of time, organise the children into apparatus groups and ask them to set out the apparatus as shown in Figure 2. (They can use either of the two layouts shown, depending on which is more appropriate for the space available.) Remind them about good lifting and careful placing (see page 42).

Ask the children in each group to disperse themselves around their apparatus, choosing a starting point as far away as possible from anyone else. Ask the children to find places where they can balance on or over the apparatus. When they have found a balance and held it for at least three seconds, they should travel to the next piece of apparatus using their feet as little as possible – for example, by rolling or taking weight on hands.

After the children have had time to explore places to balance and ways of balancing, ask them to select their best three balances and use a different piece of apparatus for each one. Allow time for the children to develop their ideas. Then ask them to go to their first piece of apparatus and demonstrate their first balance, then move on to their second balance, then to their third balance. (All the children in each group should work simultaneously, using the apparatus in rotation.) Now ask the children to return to their starting point and repeat all three balances, exploring interesting ways of linking them and moving into and out of their balances.

Allow sufficient time for practice, then ask each group to demonstrate to the rest of the class. Make sure that the children display good starting and finishing positions. The rest of the class, when observing, should be told to focus upon the requirements of the task: are three balances included in each sequence?

Conclusion

As a contrast, ask the children to refine and perform their three different jumps from the previous week, concentrating on height and controlled landings.

Figure 2

PHYSICAL
EDUCATION

Suggestion(s) for extension

Set a more demanding task for those children requiring greater challenge – for example, twisting into balance.

Group more able children together in one apparatus group. Expect them to make decisions about their apparatus layout. For example, put out the bench and mat as shown in Figure 3. Then ask them to decide where to place two hoops and two ropes. Make sure they check their layout for safety as a movement pathway. Is it well-spaced to avoid congestion?

Suggestion(s) for support

With children who are less confident, be prepared to give more direct guidance about appropriate balance points and locations – for example, 'Balance here on one foot.'

Assessment opportunities

Observe how well the children construct fluent sequences of movements around the apparatus. How well do they work individually within a group? Do the children stay on task? Are they able to set out their apparatus responsibly?

Reference to photocopiable sheet

Photocopiable sheet 117 describes a selection of warm-up activities (see page 42).

(Free Movement Pathway)

1. Put out the bench and mat.

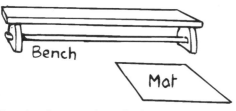
Bench
Mat

2. Decide where to place the hoops and ropes.

3. Check your layout. Is it safe?

(Free Movement Pathway)

1. You are going to plan a layout.

2. You have: one mat
one bench
two hoops
two ropes.

3. Is it a safe layout?

Figure 3

Y4 & Y5 (P5 & P6) – LESSON 1

To be introduced to partner work. To develop co-operation skills. To develop evaluation skills: making comments on a partner's performance and suggesting appropriate improvements.

†† *Individual warm-up; individual and paired gymnastic activity; whole-class conclusion.*

🕐 *Warm-up 2 minutes; gymnastic activity 30 minutes; conclusion 2 minutes.*

Previous skills/knowledge needed

The children should have broad experience of sequencing-making in gymnastics, and have developed a good understanding of the principles involved.

Key background information

The emphasis should be placed on working sensibly at the task with partners and communicating ideas thoughtfully. The teacher should seek to reward pairs that repeat and refine their sequences. Demonstration by pupils should be used frequently to assist learning throughout the class.

Preparation

The teacher will need to photocopy sequence building cards 123 and 124, then cut them up for distribution to the class. The teacher may need a copy of the 'warm-up bank' activity sheet (photocopiable sheet 117).

Resources needed

Small gym mats (one per pair of children); photocopiable sheets 117, 123 and 124.

What to do
Warm-up activity

Ask the children to enter the hall as quietly as possible and sit in a space. When the class is settled, commence the warm-up. Choose a suitable activity, perhaps from the 'warm-up bank' (photocopiable sheet 117). The choice of warm-up activity will depend on the content of the lesson and the prevailing mood of the children. Follow-the-leader activities can provide an enjoyable and stimulating warm-up. For example, divide the class into six groups, each with a leader. Ask the leader to choose various ways of travelling around the hall which the rest of the group must copy.

Gymnastic activity

Now ask the children to find their own space. Issue each child with one of the two sequence building cards 123 and 124. Allow enough time for the children to practice and refine their movement sequences, then ask them to take up their starting positions and perform their sequences. When they have finished their sequences, they should hold a finishing position for three seconds and then sit on the floor.

Put the children into pairs. Ensure that they are placed with

partners of a similar ability level, for safety reasons. Working one at a time, the children should show their sequences to their partners. The observer checks that her/his partner has performed all of the actions in the sequence. Then the children change roles.

This process should be repeated, with the observers trying to make recommendations about how the sequences could be improved. The teacher can guide the observers to think about clarity of shape **or** changes of speed **or** changes of level **or** fluency and control of movements **or** extension of the body, depending on her/his own assessment of the group's needs. The list below summarises a general structure for partner work of which the teacher needs to be aware.

PARTNER WORK

Individually
Perform the sequence on the card.

In pairs
A shows partner her/his sequence.
B checks that all of the actions on the card are performed and suggests how the sequence could be improved.
B shows partner her/his sequence.
A checks that all the actions on the card are performed and suggests how the sequence could be improved.

Teacher note
Don't worry too much about the quality of the movements in the sequence on this occasion.
Reward thoroughness in checking.

Finally, ask the half of the class using sequence card 123 to perform their sequences, then the half of the class using sequence card 124.

Conclusion

Sit the children in a class circle. Ask them to follow your instructions: *Sit up very tall – back straight – chin up – point toes – stretch arms above head – arms out to sides of body – arms in front of body – hands touching knees...* and so on, holding each position for about eight seconds.

Recap with the class, through question and answer, the important qualities required for effective partner work: concentrating; listening; giving ideas and trying out ideas; being supportive and encouraging each other's efforts.

Suggestion(s) for extension
The activity as suggested allows for suitable differentiation in this lesson, with the children being organised into ability groups (pairs).

Suggestion(s) for support
For children who are less confident, devise a simpler sequence card which includes only two actions.

Assessment opportunities
Take note of how well the children co-operate and communicate with their partners. Do observers check thoroughly that all the correct actions are included in the sequence? Do they make suggestions about how their partners' sequences might be improved? Do performers listen, and try to improve and refine their performances? Do the children fulfil the tasks independently without arguing?

Reference to photocopiable sheets
Photocopiable sheets 123 and 124 each contain three identical sequence cards (see page 43 for use) relating to movement and balances. Photocopiable sheet 117 contains a selection of warm-up activities (see page 42).

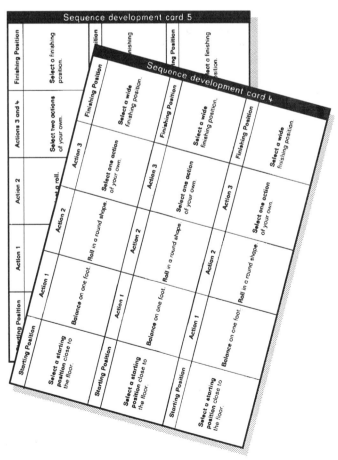

PHYSICAL EDUCATION

Y4 & Y5 (P5 & P6) – LESSON 2

To encounter the concept of matching actions with a partner. To copy a partner's sequences, matching actions side by side and then one behind the other. To develop skills in copying identical actions and synchronising those actions. To practise taking weight on hands while kicking upwards.

†† *Whole-class (paired) warm-up; paired gymnastic activity; whole-class conclusion.*

🕐 *Warm-up 2 minutes; gymnastic activity 30 minutes; conclusion 2 minutes.*

Previous skills/knowledge needed

The children will need to have substantial experience of sequence-making, and to be able to work co-operatively with a partner. They should have previous practice in taking their weight on their hands (for example, in making bunny jumps).

Key background information

The children in each pair should be of similar ability. Emphasis should be placed on the children accurately copying each other's actions and performing them at the same time as their partners. It is also worth stressing from the outset that the children should start by performing the actions slowly together, and only later introduce changes of speed.

Some movements that require mats to be performed with ease, such as backward rolls, are best organised in a side-by-side formation. (See Figure 4.) Any activity that focuses on taking the body weight on the hands, such as 'Kicking Donkeys', should only be performed for short periods of time. Watch carefully for the children becoming fatigued.

Preparation

Copies of the sequence building cards (photocopiable sheets 123 and 124) from previous work will be needed for children who were absent or who are unable to remember their sequences. The teacher will need a copy of the 'Kicking Donkeys 1' skill development card (page 125). Make sure that mats are easily accessible.

Resources needed

Gymnastic mats (one per pair of children), photocopiable sheet 125 (sheets 123, 124 and 126 may also be needed).

What to do

Warm-up activity

Explain to the class what is meant by the phrase *side by side*. Ask the children to enter the hall as quietly as possible and sit up smartly side by side with their partners.

Use a child to demonstrate with you how actions can be matched. Stand side by side with the child. Lift your right arm and ask the child to copy the action. Then see if the child can raise her/his arm at the same time and at the same speed as you. Repeat using other simple actions, until the class understands the concepts of *same action*, *same time* and *same speed*.

Ask all the children to stand side by side with their partners and perform the following matched actions:

▲ Bend at the knees – sink and rise together.

▲ Raise and lower arms together.

▲ Lift one knee together.

▲ Curl and stretch together.

▲ Stretch in a long thin shape – slowly curl, then make an identical explosive jump together.

Repeat the sequence with the partners standing one behind the other.

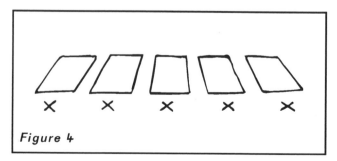

Figure 4

Kicking Donkeys 1

Start in a squat position, arms out in front of you.

Place your hands on the floor in front of your body; hands shoulder-width apart, arms locked straight. chin up.

Take your weight onto your hands, lifting hips. chin up.

Kick your heels up to touch your bottom.

Quietly return to your starting position.

Gymnastic activity

Remind the children about the sequences they have worked on before (see previous activities). Now they will perform these sequences for their partners. Ask the pairs to set out their mats in a space, one mat per pair. Remind them about good lifting and careful placing.

Now ask each pair to select two actions from each of their sequences and combine these into one joint (four-action) sequence that they can perform.

▲ Can they perform the sequence side by side?

▲ Can they perform the sequence one behind the other?

Use demonstrations to illustrate these formations when matching actions in a sequence.

Now ask the children to sit next to their mats. Introduce the 'Kicking Donkeys' activity, using photocopiable sheet 125 to reinforce good technique. Allow time for practice. Use children to demonstrate where appropriate, focusing on one teaching point at a time. The children in each pair should take turns at practising the skill on their mat.

Conclusion

Ask the children to put the mats away. Finally, sit the children in a class circle. Ask them to follow your instructions: *Sit up very tall – back straight – chin up – point toes – stretch arms above head – arms out to sides of body – arms in front of the body – hands touching knees...* and so on, holding each position for about eight seconds.

Suggestion(s) for extension

Use the 'Kicking Donkeys 2' skill development card (sheet 126) with children who are confident performers.

Suggestion(s) for support

With children who are particularly slow in developing sequences or have difficulty remembering new sequences, ask them to use one of the three-action sequences from the previous lesson and see if they can perform it side by side and then one behind the other. Alternatively pair together confident (yet supportive) sequence makers with the less confident – however, they must be at a similar achievement level of performance in the basic actions.

For the 'Kicking Donkeys' task, any child who is not ready to practise this skill should be asked to cover only the first three stages on the skill development card.

Assessment opportunities

Did the partners match their actions successfully? Could they perform a sequence at the same time?

Reference to photocopiable sheets

The sequence building cards (sheets 123 and 124) may need to be copied and cut up for children who need a reminder (or who missed a previous lesson). The 'Kicking Donkeys 1' skill development card (sheet 125) should be used by the teacher to give precise instructions to the children. 'Kicking Donkeys 2' (sheet 126) can be used for extension.

Y4 & Y5 (P5 & P6) – LESSON 3

To further develop matched sequence work with a partner. To refine combinations of 1/4, 1/2 and 3/4 turns, and to include them in a sequence (either in a side-by-side formation or one behind the other). To devise a short sequence with a partner on medium-level apparatus.

†† *Individual warm-up; gymnastic activity in pairs and groups of 6; individual conclusion.*

🕐 *Warm-up 2 minutes; gymnastic activity 30 minutes; conclusion 2 minutes.*

Previous skills/knowledge needed

The children need to have previous experience of matching work with a partner. They should have practised the 'Kicking Donkeys 1' task (see page 125).

Key background information

Rotation in the air when performing jump turns will be easier if the children adopt long thin shapes, reaching up with arms stretched. Encourage the class to spring strongly from a bent knee position. Remind them that turn jumps are a useful way of changing direction in a sequence.

Preparation

The teacher will need the skill development cards for quarter and half turns (photocopiable sheet 127) and for the 'Kicking

PHYSICAL
EDUCATION

Figure 5

Donkeys 2' task (photocopiable sheet 126). Photocopiable sheet 125 may be needed for revision. The apparatus needed should be readily accessible when the lesson begins.

Resources needed
Two gymnastic mats, one bench and one medium-level platform (small box or table) per pair, photocopiable sheets 126 and 127 (sheet 125 may also be needed).

What to do
Warm-up activity
Ask the children to enter the hall as quietly as possible and sit in a space. When the class is settled, commence the warm-up with a series of stretched jumps. Now ask the children to find their own space and all face the same direction. With their feet shoulder-width apart, they should spring up from the ground to make a long stretched shape. Whey they have made three attempts at this, ask the class to perform ¼ and ½ turn jumps. Use photocopiable sheet 127 to reinforce good technique. Allow enough time for practice. Use children to demonstrate where appropriate, focusing on one teaching point at a time.

Gymnastic activity
Ask the children to work in the same pairs as in the previous lesson, and to set out their mats in a space (one mat per pair). Remind them about good lifting and careful placing. Ask them to repeat the matched sequence they developed in the previous lesson. Then ask them to include a ¼ turn jump after the first movement. Give them time to practise this new sequence.

Then combine the pairs into apparatus groups of six children. Set out the apparatus as shown in Figure 5, with a low/medium height box or table. (They can use either of the two layouts shown, depending on the space available.) The distance from the box to the mats should encourage travelling movements. Let the groups work in their pairs to explore ways of using the apparatus when performing the actions included in their previous sequences. They should remember to include the turning jumps.

Conclusion
Ask the children to put the apparatus away. Encourage them to practise 'Kicking Donkeys 1' and then progress to 'Kicking Donkeys 2'. This is a useful practice of basic skills, which builds the children's confidence in taking their weight on their hands. Use photocopiable sheet 126 (and sheet 125, if needed) to reinforce correct technique.

Suggestion(s) for extension
Those pairs who are able to move confidently around their apparatus should be encouraged to create new, repeatable sequences of movements.

Suggestion(s) for support
Children who have difficulty in adapting their floor sequence to apparatus will require more guidance. The teacher may need to suggest pieces of apparatus which lend themselves to particular movements. It may sometimes be helpful to pair confident and less confident children together.

Assessment opportunities

Observe how well the children control their turning in the air. Do they make a long thin shape and a stable landing? Can they adapt their floor work to the apparatus setting?

Reference to photocopiable sheets

Photocopiable sheets 125 and 126 show the two 'Kicking Donkeys' skill development activities. Photocopiable sheet 127 gives instructions for quarter-turn and half-turn jumps (as well as the full-turn jump). These sheets can be used by the teacher (and by the children, if appropriate) for reference.

Y6 (P7) – LESSON 1

To explore the theme of balance further, using floor and apparatus. To explore different ways of moving into and out of balance. To link selected balances into free-flowing movement sequences. To evaluate others' sequences.

†† *Individual warm-up; gymnastic activity in apparatus groups; individual conclusion.*

⏰ *Warm-up 2 minutes; gymnastic activity 30 minutes; conclusion 2 minutes.*

Previous skills/knowledge needed

The children should have established an appropriate movement vocabulary with well-developed balancing skills on apparatus. They should be able to work responsibly and productively in apparatus groups.

Key background information

Emphasis in this lesson should be placed on the **quality of movement**. The children will need reminding to work according to their own ability, and should only attempt movements in which they feel confident. However, there may be situations where individual children want to try a particular activity which represents a high level of personal challenge. They should be encouraged to seek the help and advice of the teacher in such situations. It may be that the teacher can offer initial physical support (as a steadying influence) in developing the skill, thereby avoiding potential risk.

Apparatus layouts can be made more challenging by increasing the heights of platforms and the slopes of inclines, and by introducing more complex linking arrangements.

Preparation

The apparatus required should be dispersed around the edge of the hall for easy access.

Resources needed

Gymnastic mats, benches, boxes, platforms, large fixed apparatus (such as a climbing frame and/or ceiling ropes).

What to do

Warm-up activity

Ask the children to enter the hall as quietly as possible and sit in a space, ready to commence the warm-up. Now ask them to perform a series of turns in the air, on the spot – emphasise the need for quiet landings. Ask the class, still working in their own space, to demonstrate a series of rolls – emphasise the importance of extension and maintaining a slow speed. Can they combine their rolls and jump turns?

Now ask them to practise balances on different body parts. They should select two different balances, one of which must involve taking their weight on their hands. Now they can explore different ways into and out of their balances, such as twisting into a balance and rolling out of it.

Figure 6

Figure 7

Gymnastic activity

Organise the class into apparatus groups of like ability, and ask them to set out their apparatus. This enables groups to be allocated to appropriately challenging apparatus layouts, a progressive selection of which are illustrated here (see Figures 6, 7, 8, 9, 10 and 11). Ask the children to investigate

PHYSICAL EDUCATION

Suggestion(s) for extension

More able groups should be allocated a more complex apparatus layout, perhaps involving multiple items.

Suggestion(s) for support

Less confident children should be guided towards balances which use a large base and involve several body parts for support. Two examples are shown below.

Assessment opportunities

Observe how well the children combine their movements and balances into a sequence. Can they hold their balances still and move out of them smoothly?

Do the children co-operate effectively when they are sharing apparatus? How well do they handle the apparatus? Can each group collect and put away apparatus carefully and efficiently?

ways of balancing **on** and **against** their apparatus. Ask them to find ways of using their apparatus to help them balance, particularly when taking their weight on their hands, and then to select three balances using three different pieces of apparatus. They should try to make their movement into and out of each balance as interesting as possible, for example by making bridge shapes (see illustration below).

Make sure that each member of a particular group adopts a different place to start. Ask the children to make a sequence around their apparatus, including their three balances. Encourage them to use their feet as little as possible when travelling between items of apparatus (they can do this by rolling and sliding). They should repeat and refine these sequences, with emphasis on changes of speed within the sequence. Ask each group to demonstrate in turn, while the rest of the class evaluate the different movements.

Conclusion

Ask the class to put the apparatus away quietly, and then to practise floor sequences involving rolling and turning. This is a useful consolidation of the warm-up activity.

Y6 (P7) – LESSON 2

To practise jumping skills from apparatus, focusing on resilient landings, elevation and extension in the air. To develop partner work skills further, using large apparatus.

♦♦ *Individual warm-up; gymnastic activity in apparatus groups and in pairs; individual conclusion.*

🕐 *Warm-up 2 minutes; gymnastic activity 35 minutes; conclusion 2 minutes.*

Previous skills/knowledge needed

The children should have experience of counterbalance using partner support. They should have a well-developed movement vocabulary involving large apparatus.

Key background information

The quality of the movement sequences will depend on:
▲ contrasts in speed;
▲ contrasts in level;
▲ changes in direction;
▲ clarity of shape;
▲ smooth linking of actions (fluency).

Preparation

The apparatus needed should be dispersed around the edge of the hall ready for access.

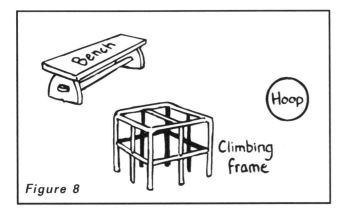

Figure 8

Figure 9

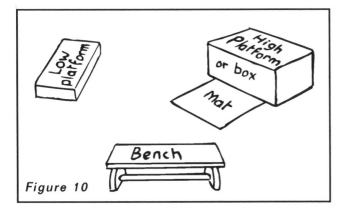

Figure 10

Figure 11

Resources needed

Gymnastic mats, benches, boxes, large fixed apparatus (such as a climbing frame and/or ceiling ropes).

What to do

Warm-up activity

Ask the children to enter the hall as quietly as possible and sit in a space. When the class is settled, start the lesson with a series of stretched jumps from the floor. Look for height and an extended body shape in the air.

Gymnastic activity

Now organise the children into apparatus groups. Ask them to set out benches and mats as shown in Figure 12. Then ask each group to use a directed movement pathway (see the figure) around the apparatus. Stress that they may only jump when the landing area is free. Ask individual children to demonstrate jumps off the bench, emphasising spring, using arms to assist lift and landing with good control. Allow time for practice, then ask the children to demonstrate various body shapes in the air: wide, tucked, long and so on.

Now ask each apparatus group to modify its apparatus layout, adding extra items of equipment. The apparatus layouts shown in Figures 6–11 may be useful for this.

Allow sufficient time for the children to rehearse previously learned movement sequences, involving linked balances, on the apparatus. Then they should work in pairs, each partner observing the other's sequence and then imitating it. Each child should tell her/his partner which parts of the sequence he/she thinks are worthy of inclusion in a joint sequence;

they should work together to reach an agreement on which are the best movements.

The teacher now sets the following task: *With your partner, devise a sequence which must include (a) a balance using apparatus; (b) a balance using your partner; (c) a jump showing elevation and soft landing; (d) contrasts in speed.* This work will take some time, probably over several lessons. When the sequences have been refined and practised, the pairs should demonstrate them to the class.

Conclusion

Ask the children to put the apparatus away. Conclude the lesson with combined jumps and rolls, performed very slowly, as a consolidation of the warm-up activity.

Suggestion(s) for extension

As partners are matched in ability, their responses to the task set will allow for a differentiated outcome.

Suggestion(s) for support

If children have difficulty in constructing partner sequences, restrict the sequence to two or three movements.

Assessment opportunities

Observe how much elevation the children achieve when jumping. How long are they able to stay in the air? Do they land under control, with knees slightly bent and still?

Observe the children's ability to combine previously learned movements into a complex sequence. Do they communicate effectively with their partners to fulfil the task?

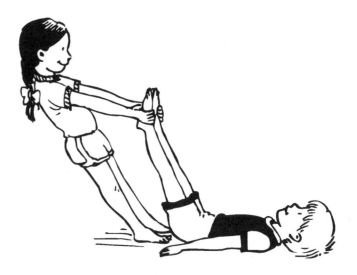

Y6 (P7) – LESSON 3

To practise jumping skills with a partner, synchronising take-offs and landings. To refine movement sequences with a partner, using large apparatus.

†† *Paired warm-up; gymnastic activity in apparatus groups; individual conclusions.*

🕐 *Warm-up 2 minutes; gymnastic activity 30 minutes; conclusion 2 minutes.*

Previous skills/knowledge needed:
The children should have explored the task: *Devise a sequence which must include (a) a balance using apparatus; (b) a balance using a partner; (c) a jump showing elevation and soft landing; (d) contrasts in speed.* (See page 53.)

Key background information
To produce movement sequences of good quality, the children will need reminders of the factors that characterise effective performance (see page 52).

To motivate the children to keep repeating and refining their work, give them plenty of opportunities to perform their sequence to the class. Motivation will be further increased if the children know they will be required to perform their work to a wider audience (such as a group of parents).

Preparation
Disperse the apparatus required around the edge of the hall for ready access.

Resources needed
Gymnastic mats, benches, boxes, large fixed apparatus (such as a climbing frame and/or ceiling ropes).

What to do
Warm-up activity
Ask the children to enter the hall as quietly as possible, form pairs and sit in a space. Set the task: *Make a sequence of three jumps on the floor with your partner, taking off and landing at the same time.* Allow the children about 10 minutes to work on this. Then ask one half of the class to demonstrate their sequences while the other half observe, looking for synchronised landings. Swap round and repeat.

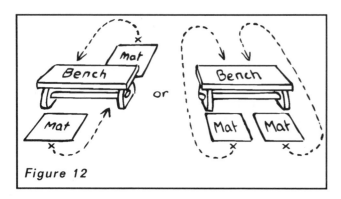

Figure 12

Gymnastic activity
Organise the children into apparatus groups and ask them to set out the apparatus. (Some possible layouts are shown in Figures 6–11.) Remind the children of the task previously set and repeat it: *Devise a sequence with your partner which must include (a) a balance using apparatus; (b) a balance using your partner; (c) a jump showing elevation and soft landing; (d) contrasts in speed.* Allow sufficient time for the children to practise their responses.

Then break down the sequence into its component parts, and ask the children to improve each component before reassembling the complete sequence. Ask each group to demonstrate their work to the rest of the class – they should bear in mind that three pairs will be working at the same time, which may require some compromise on pathways.

Conclusion
Ask the children to put the apparatus away. Conclude the lesson with children performing individually in their own space, a series of jumps, rolls and balances performed slowly to appropriate music (for example, 'Albatross' by Fleetwood Mac). Music gives variety to gymnastics lessons, and is an enjoyable and stimulating way to finish.

Suggestion(s) for extension
Confident pairs of children could add more actions to their sequence and demonstrate this version to the class.

Suggestion(s) for support
For children experiencing difficulty in constructing sequences, more time may be needed before they feel ready to perform to the rest of the class. Beware of exposing less confident children to class scrutiny until they feel assured about the quality of their work.

Assessment opportunities
Observe how well each child is able to synchronise her/his activity with that of her/his partner. Are the children prepared to go through sustained practice in working on a sequence?

PHYSICAL EDUCATION

Dance

Dance can provide a range of exciting and creative opportunities for children to express their thoughts and feelings through movement. It is often a natural extension of work in the classroom, and in this sense has the potential to make a significant contribution to overall learning.

Dance education is essentially concerned with three elements: **planning, performing and evaluating.**

Planning in this context is the art of making and devising dances, and might include at various times exploring, selecting, repeating and refining a collection of movements and actions in response to a theme or stimulus.

Performing is dancing! Components of performance include: developing and consolidating physical skill and poise; understanding the intention, form and style of a dance; sensitivity to the accompaniment and/or stimulus; using space effectively and being aware of other performers; and developing fluency.

Evaluating is making judgements and decisions about the qualities displayed in dance. It will involve observing, recognising, describing, comparing and contrasting, evaluating and responding.

Dance lessons should seek to involve children actively in all three elements; but a different emphasis will be placed on composing, performing or appreciating in line with the lesson's learning objectives. Whether the children work individually, in pairs or in groups of various sizes will also be determined by the planned outcomes of the lesson or unit of work.

PHYSICAL
EDUCATION

The dance lesson

Every dance lesson needs to embrace an idea – what is the dance about? – and this idea will need an appropriate stimulus (see below). The dance lesson also needs a **structure**, which could be as follows:

1. Warm-up activity

Warm-up activities should be related as far as possible to the rest of the lesson. This phase of the lesson should not be prolonged, however; five minutes is usually sufficient to raise the body temperature, mobilise the joints and stretch out the muscles. This preparation will help to prevent strains during the main activity.

2. Development and exploration of the main theme

This phase of the lesson will provide opportunities for pupils to expand their movement vocabulary and improve the quality of their actions, while exploring a range of movement responses to the stimulus. It may be heavily teacher-directed, or left more open-ended with the pupils themselves providing much of their own interpretation of a dance theme. The ability of the class will usually determine which of these learning strategies is the appropriate one.

The following framework represents the ingredients of a **movement vocabulary** which will help the pupils to understand, analyse and discuss their particular dance, or sections of their dance, when they are planning, composing and evaluating.

```
┌─────────────────────────────────────────────┐
│                                               │
│              What (Action)                    │
│                                               │
│  Where (Space)   INTENTION   How (Dynamics)   │
│                                               │
│              Who (Relationships)              │
│                                               │
└─────────────────────────────────────────────┘
```

▲ The **Intention** provides the starting point, and the class will need to be given time in which to think about what their dance is about and what effects they want to create.

▲ **'What' (or Action)** refers to what the body does. There are five basic actions: travelling, jumping, balancing, turning and gesture. There are three 'body' actions: bending, twisting and stretching. All these actions can be performed using a variety of body parts, shapes and body surfaces.

▲ **'Where' (or Space)** locates the dance in terms of levels, directions, pathways, zones (in front and behind), personal space (on the spot) and general space.

▲ **'How' (or Dynamics)** describes the effort put into a particular phrase or action – for example, is it sustained or sudden? fast or slow? strong or light?

▲ **'Who' (or Relationships)** establishes the context of the dance in terms of interaction with others or objects – alone, with a partner, with a group and so on.

3. Dance activity

This phase of the lesson requires the pupils to adopt a more focused approach in selecting and refining those previously-explored movements and actions which they think are appropriate to the theme and assembling them to make their dance.

4. Concluding activity

This usually involves bringing the whole class together for some gentle stretching activity, while engaging the pupils in discussion (where appropriate) about further development of their work.

The Year 3/P4 lessons in this chapter were inspired by material devised by Bob Merrell and included in *Planning Dance Lessons* by Lynda Coles (Trafford Metropolitan Borough, 1995). This is an excellent resource pack for dance at Key Stages 1 and 2.

Safety in dance

Dance lessons raise fewer safety concerns than other areas of the physical education curriculum. However, teachers should ensure that:

▲ The working space is clear and free from hazard.

▲ The floor is clean and well-maintained, particularly when the children are working in bare feet.

▲ Some form of warm-up is undertaken at the start of the lesson – make sure that the emphasis is upon stretching movements and not bouncing movements.

▲ If the children are using artefacts – as in the French stick dance, for instance, – make sure that they have enough space and skill to perform safely.

Key Stage Progression

Progression in dance over the key stage involves more complex demands being made of the children's movement vocabulary.

Dance

Year 3 (P4)

▲ **What.** Different combinations of feet used to travel: two to one, one to the other, one to the same, one to two feet, two to two feet. Tracing shapes and patterns with hands, feet and other body parts while travelling. Linking 'like' actions such as different jumps or balancing on different body parts. Linking 'unlike' actions such as travelling, jumping, balancing.
▲ **How.** Contrasting strength of different movements, such as tiptoe and stride. Showing an even flow when linking from one dance action to another.
▲ **Where.** Showing contrasts in levels: high and low.
▲ **Who.** Individually, with a partner ('copy' and 'lead and follow') and as part of a larger group.

Year 4 (P5)

▲ **What.** Travelling, jumping and balancing, focusing on contrast of body shapes. Repeating step patterns in pre-determined pathways. Highlighting pauses with held body shapes. Smooth linking of different actions. Developing 'body actions' of stretching, bending and twisting.
▲ **How.** Making contrasts of speed and strength, such as strong take-off/light landing when jumping.
▲ **Where.** More complex pathways. Awareness of medium height level. Moving in and through levels.
▲ **Who.** Individually, with a partner (matching, meeting and parting).

Year 5 (P6)

▲ **What.** More complex combinations of actions performed with greater control. Different kinds of step combinations such as step-hop, skip-step-hop.
▲ **How.** Maintaining the same speed/strength within a series of dance actions. Using repetition to establish rhythm.
▲ **Where.** Using personal space and general space.
▲ **Who.** Composing with a partner, teaching actions to a partner and performing together. Working with a partner and in fours as part of a larger group.

Year 6 (P7)

▲ **What.** Using combinations of basic actions, 'body actions' and body shapes to suggest characters or moods and feelings. Selecting dance actions to express a character. Greater control of isolated body parts.
▲ **How.** Increasing and reducing speed/strength within simple or combined dance actions.
▲ **Where.** Using gestures in different areas and levels while on the spot and to initiate travel.
▲ **Who.** With a partner, in a group and as a whole class performing to a specific audience.

A time to dance

The following dance lessons offer suggestions about how elements of dance might be delivered at various points in the key stage.

As much of dance is essentially a creative process, it is sometimes difficult to assume hard and fast periods of time in which the stated goals might be accomplished. Progress is dependent upon the response of the children in terms of their imagination and ability to translate a stimulus into a dance – this cannot be hurried. A few weeks' work in dance for some children may well represent a whole term's work for others.

Though possibly more predictable, the more formalised elements of dance – such as folk dance – still present difficulties when trying to allocate suitable periods of time, since the time needed to establish a sense of rhythm often varies considerably from child to child. With this in mind, suggestions given for the number of sessions and the duration of each session should be flexibly interpreted, particularly in those lessons where children are composing and planning responses to a stimulus themselves. Be responsive to the needs of individual children in guiding the work of a group or class.

There are many styles of dance – ethnic, country, contemporary, jazz and so on; and the teacher will need to make decisions about the type of dance to be taught. For example, is the dance required to tell a story in a dramatic form, or to express a comic theme? Will it be a more abstract dance about movement itself? Clearly, the type of dance will determine the suitability of the stimulus. It would be inappropriate, for instance, to ask children to compose a comic dance around extracts from Beethoven's Seventh Symphony.

The range of stimuli from which teachers can choose is very broad, and might include:
▲ **Music.** Music presents such a rich and varied source for setting mood and style that it is inevitably used as the most frequent stimulus for dance.
▲ **Percussion.** This can be used effectively to develop a sense of rhythm. It can also be used to suggest particular movement qualities – for example, banging a tambourine will encourage a very different movement response from shaking it. Percussion is also particularly appropriate for some ethnic dances, such as Asian and Afro-Caribbean dances. Drum beats, shakers, bells and so on can all be used to good effect.
▲ **Sounds.** These come from a variety of sources. Natural sounds (such as a rain forest), mechanical sounds, ethnic chants and so on can all be used as starting points for composition.
▲ **Ideational.** Dances can originate through ideas or themes, such as ingredients in a recipe, a firework display, or (perhaps most frequently in the primary school) the narrative of a story. Poetry can also be used as a starting idea. Even simple action words such as 'slither' or 'wriggle' may provide appropriate themes.
▲ **Visual.** Cartoons, silent movie characters, photographs, sports illustrations, fashion and animals represent a tiny sample of the potential source material.

Y3 (P4)

To explore, select and refine actions to make a dance with a clear beginning, middle and end. To interpret a poem, expressing mood and feeling through movement. To develop smooth linking of balances using turns and steps. To work as part of a group.

†† *Working in pairs and in fours.*

🕐 *Three sessions of about 35 minutes each.*

Previous skills/knowledge needed

The children should have experience of making a sequence with different body shapes, and of composing and performing with a partner. They should know about the working and living conditions of people in a northern mill town early in the twentieth century.

Preparation

Read the poem on photocopiable sheet 128 with the children a number of times, until they are familiar with the rhythm and can express in their voices some of the feeling and moods evoked by the poem. They could be given copies of the poem; or an enlarged copy on the wall could serve as a reminder. Set out a CD or cassette player. Acquire the album *The Slokar Trombones*, track 1 'Fighting trombones' and track 7 'Summertime' (Claves CD 50-711, SKC Ltd, 1987). Alternatively, the teacher can choose an appropriate selection of fast, bouncy music and slower, melodic pieces.

Resources needed

Copies of photocopiable sheet 128, a CD or cassette player, a recording of *The Slokar Trombones* or other appropriate music (see above), some photographs or illustrations of life in northern mill towns at the start of the twentieth century.

Key background information

The warm-up activity of skipping on the spot and then travelling is repeated to two different pieces of music. The first piece suggests that the weight aspect (**how**) of the movement should be lively and carefree; the second suggests that it should be weary and languid. Later in the lesson, when the poem is used as a stimulus, one of the moods that the children will be trying to express is tiredness.

The poem does not need to be interpreted literally, word for word. The children will need to have a knowledge and understanding of its subject matter from their work in humanities, so that they are able to translate the atmosphere and images into their general movements. (See the National Curriculum for England and Wales, History Key Stage 2, Study Unit 3a; Scottish National Guidelines, Social Subjects Levels C–E.) This lesson is a model of using poetry and classroom activities to support dance.

What to do

Warm-up activity

Ask the children to enter the hall quietly and sit in space. Now ask them to skip on the spot. Remind them about the different pathways we can make when travelling. Ask them to skip around the room, weaving past one another.

Now ask them to skip on the spot for 16 counts and then travel (weaving) for 16 counts – then repeat the sequences. Introduce the first piece of music: 'Fighting trombones'. Now repeat the same sequence to the second piece of music: 'Summertime'. Sit the children down with you and ask them to suggest words that might describe how they moved to each of the pieces of music.

Dance activity

Ask the children to sit in pairs. Give out copies of the poem. Read it through with the children, checking that they can recognise and remember the rhythm. Ask the children to work in pairs to explore and select two balances in different shapes to resemble the landscape and the buildings (sloping roofs, the factory, the houses, the rolling countryside, the valley). When they have developed their two balances, they should combine with another pair. Each pair will now teach the other couple their balances, so that they have a total of four balances per group. The teacher reads out the first two verses. The groups explore how to move from balance to balance, in time with the rhythm of the poem.

Now allow the children time to find ways of smoothly linking their balances. Ask them to think about using turns and single steps. Initially, the teacher should read the poem out repeatedly, so that the children can modify their linking actions in time with the rhythm. Later, they may wish to read it out themselves in order to alter the rhythm.

Ask the children (still working in groups of four) to look at different ways of travelling across the floor – for example, weaving in and out, making floor patterns based on the weaving of cloth. Then ask them each to make an individual

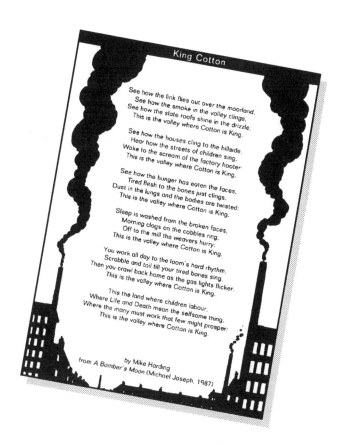

King Cotton

See how the link flies out over the moorland,
See how the smoke in the valley clings,
See how the slate roofs shine in the drizzle.
This is the valley where Cotton is King.

See how the houses cling to the hillside,
Hear how the streets of children sing,
Wake to the scream of the factory hooter.
This is the valley where Cotton is King.

See how the hunger has eaten the faces,
Tired flesh to the bones just clings,
Dust in the lungs and the bodies are twisted:
This is the valley where Cotton is King.

Sleep is washed from the broken faces,
Morning clogs on the cobbles ring,
Off to the mill the weavers hurry:
This is the valley where Cotton is King.

You work all day to the loom's hard rhythm,
Scrabble and toil till your tired bones sing,
Then you crawl back home as the gas lights flicker.
This is the valley where Cotton is King.

This the land where children labour,
Where Life and Death mean the selfsame thing,
Where the many must work that few might prosper:
This is the valley where Cotton is King.

by Mike Harding
from *A Bomber's Moon* (Michael Joseph, 1987)

Suggestion(s) for support

Make sure that all children have access to the poem by providing alternative means of communication, such as large print, tape recordings of the poem or photographs.

Assessment opportunities

Observe how well the children translate the poem into action. How well do they express the moods of the poem in their sequences? Do they link their balances smoothly? When dancing in groups of four, do they collaborate effectively? Do they contribute to discussion and share their ideas?

Reference to photocopiable sheet

Photocopiable sheet 128 contains a poem which should be read to the children, then given to them as a basis for developing movements and balances. It could be presented in other ways (see 'Suggestion(s) for support').

Y3 & Y4 (P4 & P5)

To develop basic step patterns in dance, working to a simple rhythm. To create their own dances using a common step pattern.
†† *Working individually and with a partner.*
🕐 *At least three 30-minute lessons.*

Previous skills/knowledge needed

The children should be able to hop and skip to a rhythm.

Key background information

The ability to perform simple step patterns in dance will in itself provide the children with a sense of achievement. However, a useful foundation is also being laid on which to build the more complex actions associated with (for instance) folk and ethnic dance at a later stage.

sequence of their pathways. Allow time for them to explore and develop ideas.

Now ask the children to form a group sequence which involves moving *over*, *under* and *through* each other's body shapes. Ask them to put these two sequences together.

Ask the children to sit down with you. Read to them the lines in the poem which express the feelings, appearance and movement characteristics of the workers. Pick out words such as 'tired', 'twisted' and 'crawl'. Now ask the children if they can travel, showing these movement qualities, in the sequences they have already made. Allow them time for further practice, then read verses 3 and 4 to the class as they perform their sequences. Ask them to move in time with the rhythm.

Finally, ask the children to perform the entire dance:
▲ verses 1 and 2 – their linked balances;
▲ verses 3 and 4 – their travelling sequences;
▲ verses 5 and 6 – repeat their linked balances.

Then allow each group in turn to perform its dance as the other class members read out the poem.

Conclusion

Ask the children to sit in their own space, then to repeat the warm-up activity: skip on the spot (16 counts); then skip around the room, weaving past one another (16 counts); then repeat. Use 'Fighting Trombones' to set the rhythm.

Suggestion(s) for extension

There are opportunities for children to work at their own level throughout this lesson. Groupings should be of mixed ability.

PHYSICAL EDUCATION

Preparation

Make sure that the children can hop and skip with confidence and control. Revision of these basic skills may be helpful. Set up a CD or cassette player, and obtain recordings of music suitable for a rapid step activity (such as marching bands). Provide several recordings, so the children can choose one to work with.

Resources needed

A tambourine or a drum and drumstick, a cassette or CD player, recordings of suitable music (see above).

What to do

Warm-up activity

Warm up the class with hopping and skipping in their own time (in the musical sense of this phrase). When you call 'Change!' the children must change from hopping to skipping or vice versa. Now introduce an 8-beat rhythm using the tambourine or drum. Ask the children to skip to the rhythm.

Dance activity

Ask the children to perform the following sequence: Step: Hop: Step: Hop as follows. Start with both feet together. 1. Step forward. 2. Feet together. 3. Hop on right leg. 4. Feet together. 5. Step. 6. Feet together. 7. Hop on left leg. 8. Feet together. Let the children consolidate this sequence in their own time. It may be helpful at first to restrict the sequence to the simpler version 1. Step. 2. Together. 3. Hop. 4. Together. When the children have mastered this, ask them to repeat it around the room. Then let them practise performing the step pattern to an 8-beat rhythm.

Now ask the children to work in pairs, standing next to their partners and trying to match each other's movements through the step sequence. This should be practised first in their own time, then to the 8-beat rhythm.

Conclusion

Ask the children to make up their own paired dances to a suitable piece of music using the step sequence. They might start back to back, or facing each other at a distance.

Suggestion(s) for extension

More confident children could work as a group of four when making up their own dance.

Suggestion(s) for support

Children having difficulty in co-ordinating their hopping and stepping should be encouraged simply to skip to the rhythm.

Assessment opportunities

Observe how well the children are able to co-ordinate the step pattern. Are they able to perform it to the rhythm? How imaginative are they when improvising their own dances? How well do they collaborate in the paired dances?

Y4 & Y5 (P5 & P6)

To develop travelling actions, with emphasis on stepping. To develop partner work skills, creating and performing dance patterns. To move in time to folk or traditional music that has a steady rhythm.

†† *Working in pairs and in fours.*

🕐 *Three lessons of about 35 minutes each.*

Previous skills/knowledge needed

The children should have experience of walking and stepping to a rhythm – forwards, backwards and sideways.

Preparation

Select a recording of folk music or traditional music that has a steady rhythm. You will need to be familiar with the step patterns that make up the core movements of the chorus (see photocopiable sheet 129). Make one copy per child of photocopiable sheets 129 and 130.

Dance

Resources needed

A CD or cassette player and a CD or cassette of suitable music (see above), a tambourine and stick, photocopiable sheets 129 and 130.

Key background information

After the children have become confident in performing the movements for the chorus, they may need some help in devising and combining their own step patterns for the verse. They will need an opportunity to discover how far they can travel (in 32 counts) before returning for the chorus.

What to do

Warm-up activity

Ask the children to enter the hall as quietly as possible and sit in space. Then ask them to stand, all facing in the same direction. Walk through with them:

▲ 8 steps forwards – 8 steps backwards – repeat.
▲ 8 steps backwards – 8 steps forwards – repeat.

Encourage counting and anticipating the change of direction by repeating the exercise with a skipping action.

Put on the music. Highlight the starting beat: ask the children to count and step forwards to the rhythm. Make the task more complex by adding different directions and varying the number of steps taken, using a count of 16 to return to the starting position each time.

Figure 1

Dance activity

Now ask the children to find a partner, then find another pair and sit on the floor in a group of four. The pairs should label themselves Pair 1 and Pair 2. Each group of four should find a space and sit in a square: Pair 1 facing the teacher at the front of the hall, Pair 2 with their backs to the teacher. This is the starting position. Now each pair turn to either left or right and skip or step, one child behind the other, for a count of 32 beats (the teacher strikes a tambourine to count the beat) to return to their starting position. (See Figure 1.)

Now, with Pair 1 facing Pair 2, teach the children a step pattern for the chorus, using one or more of the options shown on sheet 129 ('Step patterns'). Using a stick to strike the tambourine, encourage the children to count the beats while performing each step pattern. Then use the taped music and ask the children to perform the chorus movements three times. Explain to them that after the chorus has been performed, each couple are going to make up their own steps for the verse to the count of 32 (when they must have returned to

their starting positions). Remind the class that they can use repetition. It may be helpful to suggest and demonstrate the partner activities shown on sheet 130 ('More patterns') to the class as possibilities.

The teacher should use the tambourine and stick to count 32 beats for the children to practise repeatedly. When the children have created their own step pattern, ask them to try it to the music. Playing the tape, ask them to take up their starting positions and then: perform the chorus; add their created patterns; repeat the chorus. Ask half the class to sit down and observe the rest of the class working. The observers should check that the pair they are observing return to the starting position each time for the start of the chorus. Repeat with the other half of the class acting as observers.

Conclusion

End with a contrasting cool-down activity. Ask the children to stand in a large class circle; stretch their arms high above their heads and hold in an extended position for a count of 6; slowly curl down so that their hands touch the floor and hang in a relaxed position for a count of 6; then repeat.

Suggestion(s) for extension

Those children who display confidence in counting, stepping and co-ordinating their movement should work in groups of eight for the chorus and in groups of four when creating their own step patterns.

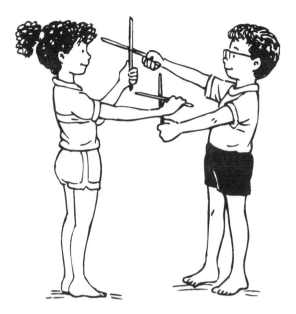

Suggestion(s) for support

Make sure that children who experience difficulty in co-ordinating their movements work with a sympathetic partner.

It would also help children who lack confidence in counting or in keeping to a rhythm to repeat simpler foot patterns rather than attempt complex and varied responses.

Assessment opportunities

Observe how well the children keep to the rhythm and return to starting positions for the chorus. Can they reproduce their foot patterns? Do they co-ordinate their own movements with those of their partner and dance group? How effectively did they work in pairs to plan their routines?

Reference to photocopiable sheets

Photocopiable sheet 129 details a number of step patterns which the children could perform for the 'chorus'. Sheet 130 details a further variety of step patterns which they could use to build up movement sequences for the 'verse'.

Y5 & Y6 (P6 & P7)

To gain experience of a dance from another culture.

†† *Pairs and small groups.*

🕐 *At least three 30-minute lessons.*

Previous skills/knowledge needed

The children should be able to perform simple step patterns. They should have some knowledge of the traditional costume, celebrations and festivals of French Basque culture.

Key background information

Dance can help children to understand their own culture and those of other countries. It can offer practical reinforcement of work undertaken in geography and the humanities, and this should be reflected in overall curriculum planning.

Preparation

This dance can usefully be linked to work on Europe. Sticks will need to be made from one-inch-thick dowelling (length about 25cm); make sure they are well-sanded and smooth. Obtain a recording of suitable music, such as traditional French dance music.

Resources needed

A tambourine or drum, wooden sticks, a CD or cassette player, a suitable recording (see above).

What to do

Warm-up activity

Start by learning or rehearsing previously-learnt step patterns (see the lesson plan on page 60).

Dance activity

Organise the children into pairs. Ask the pairs to sit down and face each other. Demonstrate the following partner hand-clapping sequence: *1. Right hand to partner's right hand. 2. Clap. 3. Left hand to partner's left hand. 4. Clap. 5. Touch your hands behind your back. 6. Clap. 7. Right hand to partner's left and left hand to partner's right simultaneously, and hold for the count of two.*

Ask the children to practise this sequence, breaking it down into small steps as necessary. Now ask them to perform the sequence in a standing position; and then to include a stepping pattern (any of the ones learned in previous lessons) at the beginning and end of their hand sequence.

Give out the sticks, two for each child. The sequence now becomes: *1. Facing your partner, make two crosses with your sticks held against your partner's sticks – the stick held in the right hand of each partner should be held horizontally. 2. Hit your own sticks together. 3. Make crosses again. 4. Hit your own sticks together. 5. Touch your own sticks together behind you. 6. Bring your own sticks to the front again and hit them together. 7. Touch sticks with your partner – right to left and left to right – and hold for the count of two.*

PHYSICAL EDUCATION

When the children have had sufficient practice to master this sequence, let them make up their own ways of incorporating their stepping patterns into the overall stick dance, working to an 8-beat rhythm. Use suitable music.

Conclusion

Conclude the lesson with individual free skipping into spaces.

Suggestion(s) for extension

More confident children should be encouraged to work in fours and add jumps to their foot patterns.

Suggestion(s) for support

For children experiencing difficulty in co-ordinating the whole dance, restrict the step patterns to simply skipping or stepping. Following a partner will also be easier than moving in a different direction.

Assessment opportunities

Observe how well the children translate their hand-clapping to stick work. Do they combine their footwork effectively with the stick routine?

Y6 (P7)

To select and combine basic actions to express characters based on the theme of a circus. To develop partner work skills of mirroring, leading and following and 'action-reaction'. To create a dance with a beginning, middle and end.

⋔ *Working in pairs and as part of a larger group.*
🕐 *At least three 35-minute lessons.*

Previous skills/knowledge needed

Experience of composing and performing with a partner. A good vocabulary of the basic dance actions and the ability to show contrasts in the '**how**' aspect of performing actions.

Preparation

Acquire a recording of appropriate parade marching or ice dancing music. Set out a CD or cassette player. Discuss circuses, acrobats and clowns with the children, using suitable books or pictures as a stimulus.

Resources needed

Pictures or books about circuses; a CD or cassette player, a suitable recording (see above), a tambourine and stick.

Key background information

In the 'Getting ready' section of the dance, the focus will be on good timing and synchronising actions with those of the partner. In the 'Tricks' section, the focus will be on the exaggerated actions of the responding partner. In the 'Tightrope' section, the focus will be on the way that different body parts contribute to maintaining balance on a tightrope. In the 'Entrance Parade' and 'Exit Parade', the focus will be on travelling quickly and quietly into place and swinging arms and lifting knees when marching; each child will also need to retain a position in relation to the rest of the class.

What to do

Warm-up activity

Ask the children to enter the hall as quietly as possible and sit in space. Then ask them all to stand facing you. Organise the class into lines, as shown in Figure 2.

Ask the children to show you a marching action on the spot. Use the tambourine and stick to highlight rhythm. Remind them about swinging their arms and lifting their knees. Now ask the children to march around the room for a count of 16, returning to the same place. (They do not need to march together.) Repeat until the children are familiar with their position in relation to the rest of the class. Ask them to stand around the outside of the working area and, on your signal, run quickly and quietly to their own place without touching other class members. When they arrive, they should begin to march on the spot. Use the tambourine to establish a class marching rhythm. Now ask the children to move to a count of 4 as follows (see Figure 3):

x	x	x	x	x	x	x	x
x	x	x	x	x	x	x	x
x	x	x	x	x	x	x	x
x	x	x	x	x	x	x	x

Teacher

Figure 2

PHYSICAL EDUCATION

Dance

1 – stretch their arms high above their heads, making a V;

2 – make fists, then bend their elbows and bring fists to shoulder height;

3 – stretch arms to sides making an inverted V;

4 – make fists, then bend elbows and bring fists up to shoulder height.

Repeat three more times (total count of 16). Use the tambourine to assist their movements.

Now ask the children to:

1 – take one small jump (light and springy) to their right;

2 – jump return to position;

3 – take one small jump to their left;

4 – jump return to position.

Repeat three more times, using the tambourine.

Now ask the children to stand outside the working area. On your signal, they should:

a) (16 counts) Travel quickly to their starting positions.

b) (16 counts) March on the spot.

c) (16 counts) Make V stretches and fists.

d) (16 counts) Make jumps to right and left.

Repeat this sequence using the music.

Dance activity

1. The clowns getting ready. Ask the children to sit with a partner. Can they tell you what things a clown might do to get ready? For example, putting on make-up and clothes, fastening their ribbons and shoelaces. Ask them to describe how the clowns might put on their trousers. For example, lying on their backs, wriggling or rocking and rolling. Allow time for the pairs to work in a space to translate four of their own ideas into actions (each action has eight counts). Tell them that the clowns are going to get ready in front of a mirror. Partners will now mirror one another's actions (moving concurrently). Perform these actions to music.

Figure 3

2. Tricks that the clowns might play. Repeat the same process: discussing possible ideas, then the children translating their own ideas into four actions (32 counts in all). The children should respond to each other, but do not need to mirror one another's actions. Ask them to highlight changes of level where possible, and to exaggerate their responding actions. Introduce the music.

3. Tightrope walkers. Now ask the children to sit in space near to the area where they have been working with their partner. Tell them to imagine they are balancing along a tightrope (32 counts): move slowly forwards – backwards – wobbling – showing pauses – showing a held balance – sinking and rising. Allow time for the children to repeat and refine their sequence of actions.

Now the children perform the whole dance. They should start out of the working area:

A) Entrance parade: travel to starting position (16 counts).

B) March on the spot (16 counts).

C) The 'Clowns getting ready' section (32 counts).

D) The 'Tricks' section (32 counts).

E) The 'Tightrope walkers' section (32 counts).

F) Return to original starting position and march on the spot (16 counts).

G) Exit parade: travel (on foot) out of the working area.

Conclusion

To conclude the lesson, encourage the children to perform controlled stretching, curling and gentle breathing. This calms them down and allows recovery from exertion.

Suggestion(s) for extension

Children who are capable of combining complex actions in a sequence could be grouped together.

Suggestion(s) for support

Children who experience difficulty in composing a dance should be encouraged to develop one of their ideas and repeat it four times rather than produce four different ideas.

Assessment opportunities

Observe how well the children translate the themes into actions. How well do they combine actions to express character? Do they mirror their partner's actions accurately? Were they able to give form and structure to their dance by remembering each section and the overall sequence?

PHYSICAL EDUCATION

Athletics

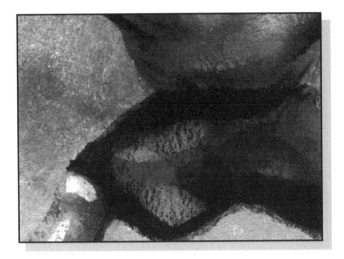

Athletics in the primary school consists of simple basic actions: running, jumping and throwing. Although in the National Curriculum for England and Wales the athletics programme of study has been removed from Key Stage 1, children will still continue to experience these basic athletic activities in games, gymnastics and dance. The same kind of activities are implicit in the Scottish 5–14 Guidelines for physical education at Levels A–B. Over Key Stage 2, the teaching task in athletics consists of developing running, jumping and throwing to be measured and judged as skills in their own right rather than as components of a specific 'athletics' programme. The KS2 Programme of Study for athletics consists of only two statements: it requires that children be taught to develop and refine the basic skills of running, jumping and throwing, and also to measure, compare and improve their performance. Though athletics remains outside the physical education core of games, gymnastics and dance, and is meant to be taught only at 'points' in the key stage, most schools will wish to include athletics as a summer activity in each year.

We tend to think of athletics in terms of highly polished competitive performance and intensive training. This may be true of athletics as a sport; but we can adopt a different view with primary children. Athletics, if taught in an appropriate manner, can provide an enriching *educational* experience for all pupils and make a significant contribution to wider goals associated with healthy lifestyle, positive attitudes and safe practice.

The athletics lesson plans

Five Key Stage 2 athletics lessons are presented in this chapter. The first two lessons represent suitable work to be undertaken in the first half of the key stage; the last three lessons are more appropriate to the second half of Key Stage 2. Additionally, a plan for a primary school sports day is outlined. This contains a series of athletics activities in a competitive form, together with photocopiable scoring sheets. Although the activities are presented in lesson form, teachers will wish to retain some flexibility in terms of how they work through the material. Many children will need longer periods of learning and consolidation than is specified in the lesson plans given. Teachers should try to include in every athletics lesson a balance between running activities (track events) and throwing/jumping activities (field events).

Each child should have a copy of the athletics record sheet (photocopiable page 131) for recording their achievements. This sheet should be maintained over the whole key stage, so that individual improvement can be recorded and followed. Opportunities should be provided at regular intervals over the summer term for the children to time, measure and record their performances in order to complete the record sheet.

The purpose of athletics in Key Stage 2

1. To promote physical activity and healthy lifestyles

The pursuit of athletic activities, with their fundamental objective of improving individual performance at whatever level, lends itself readily to teaching about physical fitness. Athletics offers children an effective practical route towards a better understanding of the three 'S's: stamina, strength and suppleness. Despite the importance of technique, there can be no doubt that an improvement in these purely physical qualities holds the key to running faster, jumping longer or higher and throwing further.

The following key questions will be useful for pupils:

▲ *What qualities do I need to run quickly over a short distance? How can I improve my speed?*

▲ *What do I need to do to improve my ability to run longer distances in less time?*

▲ *Why are strength and suppleness important in helping me to throw and jump as well as possible?*

2. To develop positive attitudes

Athletics is often seen as a highly individualised competitive activity. However, a more flexible and imaginative approach is needed with children. The following observations illustrate the broader interpretation of 'competition' needed:

▲ Success is vital in encouraging enthusiastic participation from all pupils. As well as providing opportunities to compete directly against their peers, athletics additionally allows pupils to compete against their own past achievements. Achievement can be regulated through national standards such as the 5 Star Award scheme, and provides incentives for more talented and less talented children alike.

▲ Teachers should encourage children to measure and record their own performance and those of their peers as much as possible. This helps the children to develop a sense of responsibility and an awareness that enjoyable competition is only possible when honesty and fairness prevail.

▲ The frequent use of small-side team competition in the throwing and jumping activities, as well as (more obviously) in the running relays, will encourage pupils to value their own contributions to a team effort and to support the efforts of their team-mates. Further guidance is given on the use of small-team athletic competition in the lesson material.

3. To ensure safe practice

Consideration of safe practice inevitably tends to be dominated by the throws, though potential hazards always exist on the running track and around the jumping areas. More information about safety in athletics is given opposite; but a few general points are worth reinforcing here.

From the outset, pupils will need to appreciate that certain rules relating to safety must **never** be broken. Because the implements used at primary level are relatively safe, however, the teacher will be able to place children confidently in situations where they are allowed to regulate their own activity, making for a more complete learning experience. The development of safety awareness on the part of pupils will, of course, occur more rapidly within a context of good organisation, consistency and effective teacher supervision.

Skill demands in athletics

In games, children are required to make frequent decisions about the type of response needed in order to outwit an opponent or gain control of the ball. Decision-making of this kind is less evident in athletics, with the possible exception of some of the longer-distance running events (up to 1000m) where tactics can have a bearing on the outcome. Most athletic activity (particularly throwing and jumping) is **self-paced**, with the participants themselves deciding when exactly to commence their effort rather than it being determined by the actions of opponents. Consequently, in athletics there is greater opportunity for children to think through their actions (**planning**), as when preparing to make a long jump or throw an implement. Similarly, there will usually be time after the action is completed for children to reflect meaningfully upon the merits of their performance (**evaluation**), usually with the benefit of immediate feedback. The development of more effective techniques in athletics thus becomes achievable.

It should be emphasised that primary school athletics is about developing **basic techniques**, upon which it will be possible to build more advanced and sophisticated levels of skill at a later stage. The 'sports day' lesson plan given later in this chapter, for example, contains a number of activities which accurately reflect the developmental stage of primary school children, but which are integral to the sport of athletics.

The following teaching points may be useful.

▲ **Running.** Children should be encouraged to relax as much as possible when running. When running quickly (sprinting), they should run on their toes (the ball of the foot) and work hard with their arms. For running over longer distances, a heel-toe action (the heel reaching the ground first on each stride) is more effective, with the arms kept low and relaxed.

▲ **Jumping.** When jumping for distance and height, children should use a short, slower, more controlled approach (run-up) rather than a longer or rapid one. All jumping in primary school athletics involves taking off from one foot and landing on two – with the exception of the triple jump (which involves a hop, a step and then a jump) and the standing broad jump. Jumping in athletics is slightly different from jumping in gymnastics or dance: it tends to be flat-footed at take-off.

▲ **Throwing.** Throwing in the primary school should be confined to a ball (large and small), beanbag and **foam** javelin. The approach, if used at all, should be short (no more than five strides) and controlled. The body should be sideways-on immediately prior to the throw, with the implement taken as far back as possible with the throwing arm.

Safety in athletics

The greater risks in athletics occur in the secondary school, where the type of throwing implement used and the teaching of more advanced jumping techniques make careful vigilance necessary at all times. However, primary teachers will need to be equally concerned with safe practice in athletics, addressing the current well-being of their children while establishing good safety habits which the secondary school can build upon. The following principles and rules will be useful in maintaining a safe working environment.

▲ Care must be taken in all outdoor athletic activities when the ground is wet. Throwing and hurdling should not be attempted in these conditions.

▲ Developmental considerations will need to determine the nature and type of athletic activities taught. Throwing heavy implements is not a suitable activity for children in Key Stage 2. When children are running for distance, it is recommended that 1000m is not exceeded; and longer distances must be worked up to by training over shorter distances.

▲ Although some useful work can be undertaken with children in developing a foundation for high jump technique – using a low cane, a scissors-style jump (or, indeed, any 'feet to feet' style of jump) and a minimal approach – competitive high jumping should not be pursued without the benefit of specialist resources.

When children are engaged in throwing activities, make sure that everyone remains behind the throwers and remains vigilant, and that the throwers themselves always check that their field is clear before throwing. Observers must **always** remain behind the throwing line. The implements must only be retrieved on instruction and must **never** be thrown back. It must be made clear to the children that throwing a ball in athletics carries certain responsibilities that are not so apparent in games (where ball movement is continuous and fairly predictable). It should be emphasised that whenever **any** implement (no matter how light) is thrown for distance in athletics, the above throwing rules must apply.

Key Stage 2 progression

Athletics at Key Stage 2 focuses on the **basic actions** of **running, jumping and throwing**.

Pupils should be encouraged to improve their performance through **measurement and comparison, perseverance** and **technical guidance**.

Pupils should be aware of the effects of the different athletic activities upon their physical development.

Pupils should have frequent opportunities to investigate and solve problems relating to effective performance.

Years 3 and 4 (P4 and P5)

▲ Development of running technique within a variety of competitive and non-competitive contexts, for example: running against the clock, different pathways, shuttle relays, shorter distances (such as 30m) and longer distances (such as 200m).

▲ Development of throwing techniques using a large ball and a small ball, with a stationary throwing position.

▲ Development of jumping technique, with an emphasis upon jumping for distance.

Years 5 and 6 (P6 and P7)

▲ Further development of running technique, incorporating longer distances (up to 1000m) and circular relays.

▲ Further development of throwing techniques using balls and foam javelins, with an approach run.

▲ Further development of jumping techniques to include jumping for distance, jumping for height and combination jumps (such as a hop, step and jump).

Y3 & Y4 (P4 & P5)

To develop running skills, with an emphasis on running quickly. To develop jumping for distance. To use opportunities for estimation and recording of athletic performance.

†† *Whole-class warm-up activity; paired running and jumping activities; team jumping activity in groups of 4.*

🕐 *Warm-up activity 3–4 minutes; running activity 25 minutes; paired and team jumping activities 25 minutes.*

⚠ *This activity should not be attempted on grass if the ground is wet.*

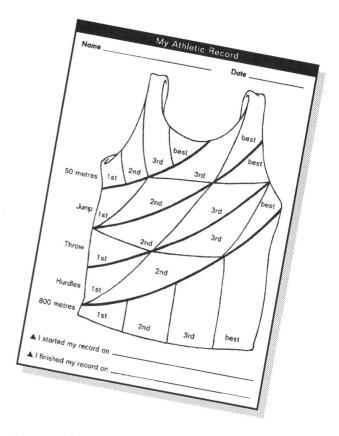

Previous skills/knowledge needed

Although there is no provision for athletics as such in Key Stage 1, the majority of pupils should be able to run and jump with confidence by the age of seven years as a consequence of their previous experience in physical education. The children should already be familiar with working co-operatively, and have developed the ability to land in a controlled manner when jumping. During this activity they will need to measure and record their performance using standard metric measures of distance.

Key background information

Teachers can employ the following teaching points in order to help the children improve the basic skills they already have:

▲ *For running quickly, the way your arms move is just as important as how your legs move; make sure your elbows are bent and work your arms quickly.*

▲ *Try to relax as much as possible.*

▲ *Lift your knees high and run on your toes.*

▲ *When jumping, bend your knees at take-off and lift up HIGH; start and finish with your feet flat on the ground.*

Preparation

Make a copy of the athletic record sheet (photocopiable page 131) for each child. They will need to have access to their record sheets at every subsequent athletics lesson throughout the key stage.

Resources

A playground or field (with a suitable starting line), beanbags, metre rules or tape measures, a stopwatch, a whistle, one athletic record sheet (sheet 131) per child, pencils.

What to do

Warm-up activity

Start the lesson with a brief warm-up (three to four minutes) involving some easy jogging and stretching.

Athletic activity 1

Organise the class into pairs: one partner running and the other observing. Ask the children to estimate how far they can run in three seconds. The running partners assemble on a start line, after placing a beanbag at the point they think they will reach in three seconds. The teacher signals the start and finish of this period using a stopwatch and whistle. The observing partner sees how accurate the estimation was by standing alongside the beanbag, then readjusts it as necessary. Let each pair have at least three attempts, then change the runners and observers over. Ask each child to mark her/his best attempt with a beanbag. This mark then serves as the child's start for a class race back to the original starting line. If this handicapping arrangement is effective, all the children should (in theory) cross the line together!

Athletic activity 2

Organise the class for a jumping activity. Ask the children to assemble on a line to practise the standing broad jump (see Figure 1). After several minutes' practice, ask them to work with a partner to measure and record their best attempt for inclusion on their athletic record. (See Figure 2).

Athletic activity 3

Finish with a team jumping activity using the standing broad jump. Organise the children

Figure 1

PHYSICAL EDUCATION

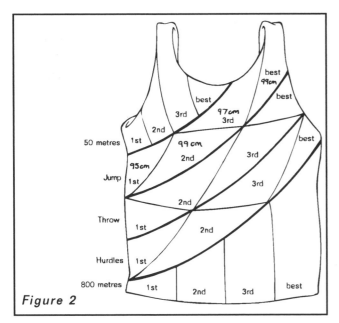

Figure 2

To develop running skills, with an emphasis on conserving energy over longer distances. To develop throwing skills further, with particular emphasis on throwing a large ball for distance.

†† *Whole class warm-up; running activity in groups of 4 or 5; throwing activities in pairs and teams of 4.*

🕐 *Warm-up 3 to 4 minutes; running activity 25 minutes; throwing activities 25 minutes each.*

Previous skills/knowledge needed

The children will need to be able to run confidently and demonstrate basic ball-handling skills. They will also need to be able to work co-operatively in pairs and small groups.

Key background information

The majority of children entering Key Stage 2 will have had little experience of sustained running, and their understanding about the need to conserve their energy when running over longer distances will be relatively limited. Children at this stage of development tend to attempt every running task (whatever the distance) at top speed. The ability to spread individual effort effectively over a longer period of time is something that teachers can help children to develop.

Although children will have spent a significant amount of time on throwing during their early years, this activity will have had control and accuracy as its main focus. The principles associated with throwing for distance, and the use of strength to achieve this, will rarely be apparent.

The following teaching points will be useful:

▲ *When running a long way, carry your arms low and keep to a steady, constant speed.*

▲ *Land on your heels with each stride.*

▲ *When throwing, try to take the ball back as far as possible – the more work you do on the ball, the further it will go.*

▲ *Always try to throw from a good balanced position, with your feet widely spaced.*

▲ *When throwing, try to keep your feet on the ground for as long as possible.*

into groups of four, with the children in each group numbered 1 to 4. All teams start on the same line, and child number 1 jumps off. Number 2 marks the landing point of number 1, then uses it as her/his starting point. This continues through the whole team and is then repeated, making a total of eight jumps (two per team member). The team finishing furthest down the playground or field wins. Using each team finishing point as its new start and reversing the direction of jumping provides a useful handicapping procedure for a subsequent competition.

Suggestion(s) for extension

In the running activity, extend the time interval to five or six seconds. The jumping activities can be made more physically demanding by asking each child to perform three consecutive broad jumps instead of just one.

Suggestion(s) for support

The handicapping arrangements described above ought to ensure that children of all abilities become involved in fair competition at some stage of the lesson. However, teachers should make sure that the teams for competition are of comparable overall ability wherever possible.

Assessment opportunities

Observe particularly how children use their arms to assist their running. In jumping, how much height (lift) do they achieve at take-off? Remember that more height means greater distance. Can the children measure each other's performance, and record their own, accurately? The record sheet (photocopiable page 131 will provide evidence of this.

Reference to photocopiable sheet

In this and all the following lessons, the 'My Athletic Record' sheet (page 131) should be used by the child to keep a record of her/his achievements and progress.

PHYSICAL
EDUCATION

Preparation

The children will need to have ready access to their current athletic recording sheets (photocopiable page 131).

Resources needed

A playground or field with a starting/throwing line, cones and/or skittles, stopwatches, beanbags, one large ball for each pair of children, tape measures, photocopiable sheet 131, pencils.

What to do

Warm-up activity

Warm up the class with some gentle jogging and stretching.

Athletic activity 1

Set out a running circuit similar to the one shown in Figure 3, using four cones or skittles (if the class is large, it may help to set out more than one circuit). The objective of the activity is for the children to run a series of 'laps' at the same speed, using 'paced' running.

Organise the children into groups of four or five. Set the first group off and time its first lap. The children should run the lap together at a steady speed. When the first group has completed its lap, the children will need to record their time. This group then rests while the other groups in turn complete a timed lap. The competition is to see which group can repeat a second lap in the same time as its first run. The team nearest to its initial time (not the fastest team!) wins.

Athletic activity 2

Organise the class into pairs for throwing. One partner throws a netball or football as far as possible from a throwing line, using a soccer throw (forward and overhead – see Figure 4.) The other partner 'marks' the best throw of three with a beanbag, which is moved as necessary. The partners then change over. Each person's best throw is measured for recording on their athletic record sheet (sheet 131).

The partners then combine with another pair to make a team of four for a team throwing competition. Six to ten skittles are set out at two-metre intervals from the throwing line. The first skittle represents one point, the second skittle two points and so on. Each child has three throws, and the points scored by the four team members are added together. The team with the highest total wins the competition.

Suggestions for extension

In the running activity, give each member of the team in turn the responsibility for leading the rest of the group and setting the pace – the 'pacemaker' role. The team throwing activity can be made more challenging by extending the distances between the skittles.

Suggestion(s) for support

It should be emphasised to the children that the running activity is a **team activity** and that the whole group should stay close together throughout the run. Children experiencing difficulty in the throwing activities may find throwing easier with a lighter, smaller ball such as a foam ball.

Assessment opportunities

Observe how well the children co-operate in the running event. Do they concentrate on the task and plan their effort? In throwing, do they demonstrate a good overall action, bringing the ball from well behind the head and releasing it at the last possible moment? Can they measure and record their performance accurately?

Reference to photocopiable sheet

The athletic record sheet (page 131) can be used by the children to record their performances.

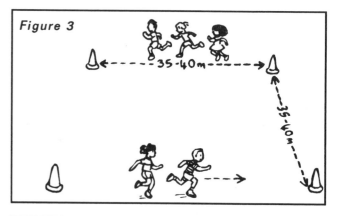

Figure 3

35-40m

35-40m

Figure 4

Y5 & Y6 (P6 & P7)

To become familiar with the baton relay race. To develop jumping skills further by combining jumps into a triple jump (hop, step and jump).

†† *Whole class warm-up activity; running activity in groups of 4; jumping activity as class and in pairs.*

🕐 *Warm-up 3–4 minutes; running activity 25 minutes; jumping activity 25 minutes.*

⚠ *Safe handling of the baton must be emphasised.*

Previous skills/ knowledge needed
The children will need to be able to run and jump with confidence and control. They will also need the capability to work co-operatively with a partner and in small groups.

Key background information
The ability to run quickly and jump with confidence and control will be demonstrated by most children towards the end of Key Stage 2. They will be able to perform these basic skills without a great deal of concentration, thus allowing 'additions' to be integrated into the action itself (as in a relay baton changeover) or a series of basic skills to be combined into a more complex sequence of actions (as in the triple jump).

In helping children to develop these more demanding athletic activities, the following teaching points will be useful:
▲ *When running quickly, always look straight ahead.*
▲ *When giving the baton, try to place it firmly into the hand of your team-mate.*
▲ *When receiving the baton, try to hold your receiving hand steady and make it as big a target as possible.*
▲ *When triple jumping, try to keep your body as high as you can throughout the sequence. There should be no pause between the hop, step and jump.*
▲ *Don't forget to use your arms in helping you lift up into the air – swing them vigorously upward with each take-off.*

Preparation
Make sure that the children have ready access to their athletic record sheets so that they can record their individual performances (distances achieved in the jumping activity).

Resources needed
Relay batons (these can easily be made from broom handles sawn into 25cm lengths and smoothed off), tape measures, record sheets (photocopiable sheet 131) and pencils.

What to do
Warm-up activity
Start with a short warm-up consisting of gentle jogging and stretching.
Athletic activity 1
Organise the class into groups of four. Mark out a straight running track of 50m. Use skittles or cones to indicate at

least six lanes (if there are no markings available) to help the children keep to straight lines (see Figure 5).

Now ask the children to run down the straight (one pupil in each lane) three or four times at about half speed, concentrating on looking ahead. Allocate each group to a lane and ask the children to space themselves out at about 10m intervals. The first child walks with the baton and at passes it on to the second child, who passes on to the third and so on. The children then reverse this process, walking in the opposite direction with number four leading off. Ask them: *What problems have you encountered in passing the baton? What do you need to do to make it easier?*

Hopefully, the children will realise that to give and receive the baton with the same hand leads to difficulties since the incoming 'runner' is likely to run into the back of the outgoing 'runner'. Ask the children, working in their groups, to find a solution to this . What should emerge is that alternate hands need to be used (right to left to right to left) in order to make room for the incoming runner and smooth out the baton exchange. Alternatively, the baton could be always received,

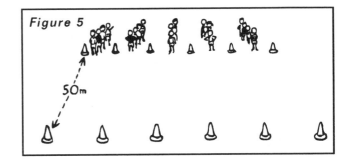
Figure 5
50m

say, in the right hand, but then transferred by each runner to the left hand before the next exchange.

The children can now progress from walking to jogging speed, which poses a new problem: when exactly does the outgoing runner set off, since to take the baton stationary will clearly make for a very slow change-over? Set the children the following task: *Now go back to your groups and investigate when and how you should signal to the person receiving the baton that he/she should set off.* The children should conclude that a shout such as 'Go!' from the incoming runner at about five strides' distance will ensure that the baton is exchanged on the move and at the right point.

Now ask the class to speed things up gradually. Don't worry about having take-over zones: simply encourage the children to exchange the baton on the run without interfering with other runners. When they can do so consistently, build in some competition. A relay race can be run in straight lines (for example, seeing which team is the first to complete 12 exchanges running up and down their straight). Alternatively, the class can transfer to a running circuit where the space is available to run a more orthodox relay race. Make sure the faster teams are allocated to the outside lanes without a stagger, so that they have further to run.

Athletic activity 2

Organise the class for a jumping activity. Line the children up on a line marking, with a good space between each child and the next. Ask them to hop forward (take off and land using the same foot). Practise this several times. Then ask them to add a step (take off from one foot and land on the other) to the hop. Practise this combination several times. Finally, add a jump (take off from one foot and land with feet together) to the hop and step. Practise this new combination several times. It will help the children to think about their feet when landing: SAME (hop) – OTHER (step) – TOGETHER (jump). This activity is best performed from a stationary position, without an approach run.

Now ask the children, working in pairs, to measure and record their best attempt from three further attempts. They can use their athletic record sheets for this.

Suggestion(s) for extension

In order to accelerate away effectively, many children will benefit from a technically sound **standing start**. (A crouch start offers little advantage without spiked shoes and starting blocks.) Figure 6 shows the main features of a standing start:

▲ arms already in running position (NB if right leg is forward, LEFT arm is forward and vice versa);

▲ a good bend at the knees;

▲ feet pointing straight down the track;

▲ weight over the front foot.

Those children who learn the triple jump combination quickly should be given the opportunity to add on a short approach run; but restrict this to no more than five strides.

Figure 6

Suggestion(s) for support

For groups that are experiencing some difficulty in passing the baton, it may be helpful to break the activity down further into a partner activity. Some children may benefit from simply running while holding their receiving hand backwards, without receiving a baton, with a partner observing whether the hand is held steady.

For children experiencing difficulty with the triple jump, allow more time to practise the hop and step without the jump. Slow the complete action down, so that the children can mentally 'programme' the next action in the sequence: HOP – pause – STEP – pause – JUMP.

Assessment opportunities

Observe how smoothly the children exchange their batons. Have they established a good way to inform the receiver? Can they handle the baton safely while running at top speed?

Can the children link the hop, step and jump into a fluent sequence? Are they able to measure each other's efforts accurately?

Reference to photocopiable sheet

The children can record their performances on the athletic record sheet (page 131).

Y5 & Y6 (P6 & P7)

To further develop tactical running over longer distances. To further develop throwing a small ball and/or foam javelin for distance.

†† *Small groups for introduction; individual warm-up; pairs within groups for running activity; throwing activity in pairs.*

🕐 *Classroom introduction 5–10 minutes; warm-up 3–4 minutes; running activity 25 minutes; throwing activity 25 minutes.*

Previous skills/knowledge needed

The children will need to have basic understanding of the need to conserve energy when running longer distances. They will also need to be able to throw a small ball with confidence and control from a stationary position.

Key background information

Towards the end of Key Stage 2, children are able to sustain their efforts for longer periods of time. As stamina levels increase, children find running longer distances an enjoyable and rewarding challenge. Their basic throwing action should be well established, and further refinement in technique becomes possible as the children try to gain extra metres when throwing for distance. The action of throwing a small ball is quite similar to that of throwing a javelin. Thus useful foundation work can be done from which the mature throwing event can easily be developed in secondary school. Primary schools can also replicate the javelin event more closely with foam javelins, which are now available from most equipment suppliers. If used with care, foam javelins are safe throwing implements which are suitable for indoor and outdoor work.

The following teaching points will be useful:

▲ *When running longer distances, try to relax and maintain a steady rhythm. Don't speed up or slow down too often.*

▲ *Keep your arms loose.*

▲ *When throwing for distance, remember that technique (a good uncomplicated action) is just as important as effort.*

▲ *A long approach is not necessary and will tire you out – five strides are usually sufficient to make a good throw.*

▲ *Remember that what you do with your legs is just as important as your arm action when throwing for distance – you must be in balance. Imagine how difficult it would be to try and throw a long way on roller skates!*

Preparation

The children will need their athletics record sheets. Provide calculators, if appropriate, for the initial problem.

Resources needed

A field or playground with a line (for throwing from); skittles or cones; stopwatches or clocks (one for each pair of children, if possible); small balls or foam javelins, tape measures; one copy per child of photocopiable sheet 131; blank paper, pencils, calculators (if needed).

What to do
Introduction

Before going outside, set the class the following problem to work on in small groups: *We are going to set out a circuit for an 800m race, using cones or skittles on the playground or field – a 50m by 50m square is suitable for this.* (See Figure 7.) *I want you to run the total distance in less than 5 minutes if possible. Try to run each of the four laps in approximately the same time. What time will you need to run each lap in?*

Discuss the children's findings. Make sure they agree that the target time for each lap is 1 minute 15 seconds. Ask them to calculate target 'running total' times for each of the four laps. When these times are agreed, move outside.

Warm-up activity

Warm up with some gentle jogging and stretching.

Athletic activity 1

Organise the class into pairs; then put the pairs into four larger groups and allocate each group to one corner of the square. One of each pair will now time while the other partner runs. It will be necessary for the 'timers' to feed information

to the runners as they pass their home skittle, using the target 'running total' times for each of the four laps. Then change the timers and the runners over and repeat.

Now ask all the children to calculate their own average time for an individual lap from their timer's recorded total time for their run. Ask them whether they maintained an even pace. Did they speed up to get nearer the target time? Did they start off too fast and get tired? Remind them of the importance of 'pacing yourself' over longer distances.

Now ask the children to set themselves realistic, but challenging, target times for the overall 800m run and break the target time down into four equal target lap times. In the next lesson, they can work in pairs to try and achieve these targets, recording the results.

Athletic activity 2

Organise the children into pairs. Ask them to stand behind a throwing line. One partner will throw and the other will observe and judge. Ask the throwers to practise several throws from a stationary position, using a small ball or foam javelin. Remind them to take the implement as far back as possible by turning their body and reaching as far behind them as possible with the throwing arm. Tell them to place their weight on the back foot and space their feet out. Partners can check that a good throwing position has been achieved. After several practice throws they change over.

Next, introduce a short approach run. Emphasise that the thrower's feet must not cross the throwing line. Partners can act as judges to see that this rule is not broken. Set the class the following problem, which they should solve by trying out different methods: *If you cannot cross the throwing line, how will you need to plan your approach run?*

The children will need to learn, through further practice, that they must prepare to throw at least two strides away from the throwing line if they are to control their forward momentum and not cross it after throwing. It will be helpful to the children if they are encouraged always to step back from the throwing line after throwing.

Now set out a series of skittles at 10m intervals from the throwing line. Ask the children to make three throws and mark them with skittles, then record their best throw on their athletic record sheet (photocopiable sheet 131).

Figure 7

PHYSICAL EDUCATION

Suggestion(s) for extension

In the running event, children with greater stamina may benefit from planning a longer run; but this should not exceed 1000m.

Encourage the successful throwers to follow through powerfully with the throwing arm. This may require the feet to 'reverse' – the back foot is brought rapidly through, taking an extra quick, small step in order to 'brake' the forward speed – in order not to cross the line.

Suggestion(s) for support

Shorten the running distance for those children who lack stamina. Children should not experience undue discomfort when running longer distances.

Assessment opportunities

Observe how well the children stick to their running plan. Do they run in a relaxed manner and maintain a steady pace?

In throwing, are the children able to integrate their approach and throwing actions, or do these still appear to be two separate movements? Are they able to measure and judge the throws of their partners reliably?

Reference to photocopiable sheet

The athletic record sheet (page 131) can be used by the children to record their performances.

Y5 & Y6 (P6 & P7)

To develop basic hurdling technique.

†† *Individual warm-up; hurdling activity as whole class, in groups and in pairs.*

⏱ *Warm-up activity 3–4 minutes; hurdling activity 45 minutes.*

⚠ *Hurdling must take place on a safe surface, preferably dry grass or playground.*

Previous skills/knowledge needed

The children will need to be able to run with confidence, and to work co-operatively with a partner.

Key background information

Children who are able to run confidently and have developed a reasonable sense of rhythm will take to this event with enthusiasm. The 'hurdles' can easily be fabricated from canes and skittles. They must be light and non-threatening: children should not be inhibited in any way from dislodging the barrier. They should see hurdling as **fast running over obstacles**, not as something resembling the high jump.

The following teaching points will be useful:

▲ *Speed is the essence of this activity – try not to slow down at any stage.*

▲ *Clearing the hurdles quickly is much more important than how much time you spend in the air.*

Preparation

Make sure that the children have ready access to their athletic recording sheets.

Resources needed

A field or playground, skittles, light canes, stop-watches (one per pair of children), chalk or beanbags, one copy per child of photocopiable sheet 131.

What to do

Warm-up activity

Start with a short warm-up activity of skipping with a high knee action.

Athletic activity

Ask the children to run across a number of regularly-spaced canes (say four over 30 metres) which are placed flat on the floor, without stepping on them. Then raise the canes onto 30cm skittles. Present the class with the problem of getting over them as quickly as possible. Ask: *Is it better to take off from one foot or two? Is it better to land on one foot or two?*

The children should arrive at the best solution – taking off from one foot and landing on the other – by timing each other. Taking off and landing on both feet acts as a brake on forward speed.

The next problem is to alter the distance between the canes such that the same leg is used for take-off each time, in order to assist rhythm and balance. Ask: *How many strides between the barriers does this require?* The children should conclude after further practice that they must make an odd number of strides between the barriers in order to take off from the same foot each time. (See Figure 8.)

Now raise the canes to about mid-thigh height. (This will require dividing the class into several groups of different ability.) Pose the problem: *How can you clear the cane without wasting time in the air?* Remember, in hurdling it is the fastest runner down the track who wins the race, not the person who jumps the highest over each hurdle.

There are several possible solutions to this problem. After a suitable period of practice, some children may see that body position in the air is important, with the trailing leg needing to be brought through parallel to the ground. The solution most worth emphasising, however, relates to the take-off. Most children will run too close to the canes and will have to jump rather than hurdle. Ask the children, in pairs, to mark each other's take-off spot and then move it a little further away from the cane (not too far at first). This will automatically have the effect of lowering the body's flight path over the cane, thus encouraging the children to drive across the cane rather than make a jump (see Figure 9).

Now set out four flights of canes on skittles at different spacings over a distance of 40m (see Figure 10). Ask the children to work on the flight that they feel most comfortable with, but encourage them to choose a flight where they are able to make three strides between the barriers when running quickly. Remind them to hurdle one way only (this will help to establish good habits which will become essential in later work using 'real' hurdles). Partners can time each other hurdling over a distance of 40m. Their achievements can be recorded on photocopiable sheet 131.

Suggestion(s) for extension
Children who display confidence in this activity might be further challenged by introducing more hurdles (no more than six) and setting them a little higher.

Suggestion(s) for support
For those children who initially find the activity difficult, practice over a single hurdle may be helpful in building confidence; but try to introduce a second hurdle as quickly as possible, since movement between the hurdles is just as important as movement over them.

Assessment opportunities
Observe how rhythmically the children move between and over the canes. The rhythm should be 'over-one-two-three-over-one-two-three-over...'. Do the children clear the canes confidently, or do they approach them hesitantly?

Reference to photocopiable sheet
The athletic record sheet (photocopiable sheet 131) can be used by the children to record their performance.

THE SCHOOL SPORTS DAY

To be involved in organising and carrying out a whole-school competitive activity. To build on the term's or year's work in PE. To observe rules of fair play.

†† *Teams of 6 to 12 children.*

🕐 *Events running concurrently over a whole day.*

Key background information
The objectives of a primary school sports day should be:
1. To involve as many children as possible as active participants in the competition. A successful sports day ideally involves every child in the school.
2. To complement and build upon the work in physical education which has taken place over the year or term.
3. To arrange events or activities which are compatible with the developmental stage of the children and represent achievable and realistic challenges for them.
4. To involve all the children in healthy competition which they perceive to be fair.

The following organisational structure will be necessary if photocopiable sheets 132 to 137 are used:

▲ **Teams.** The children should be organised into teams of between six and twelve athletes. Each team should have the same number of children, and should contain an equal number of boys and girls. This can be done on an age basis, with separate competitions for each year; or different age groups can be mixed. All the activities are very simple and are suitable for all KS2 children. While hurdling, for example, is given in the lesson plan on page 74 as a Year 5 or Year 6 (P6 or P7) activity, Year 3 and Year 4 (P4 and P5) children

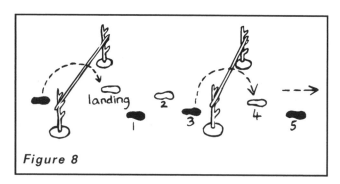

Figure 8

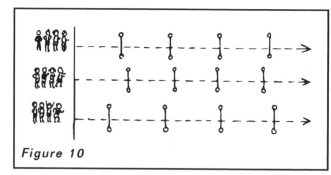

Figure 10

Figure 9

to station together. If this is the case, make sure that enough equipment is available for the teams to work simultaneously. This would also require more than one judge to be present at each station.

Reference to photocopiable sheets
Photocopiable sheet 134 shows a suggested layout for the events. Sheet 132 is an event record sheet to be used by the judge for each event. Sheet 133 is a master score sheet on which the total score of each team can be worked out. Sheets 135 to 137 detail the rules for each event.

will have covered jumping in gymnastics and should be able to participate easily in a suitably-pitched hurdle relay.

▲ **Scoring.** Teams receive points depending on the positions they achieve in each of the eight events. Thus, if there were 12 teams in your sports day, the winning team in an event would be awarded 12 points, the second team would get 11 points and so on. The scores from the eight events are totalled to find the overall winners. The scoring of individual events is described in the rule sheets (pages 135 to 137).

▲ **Judging.** Each of the eight events will need its own judge. The judge will need to complete an event record sheet for each team and send this to be entered on the master score sheet (see pages 132 and 133).

Preparation
Make sure the children understand their responsibilities as judges and team members, and are aware of the relevant issues of safety and fair play.

Resources needed
A copy of the layout sheet (photocopiable sheet 134); one event record sheet (photocopiable sheet 132) for each judge; a copy of the master score sheet (photocopiable sheet 133); copies of the rule sheets (photocopiable sheets 135 to 137); clipboards and pens or pencils; a cane with two supports, cones, tape-measures, stop-watches, foam javelins.

What to do
The teams move around the circuit in rotation, one team at a time trying each event in the sequence. Activity 9 is a rest break. The events have been arranged to space out the higher-activity ones (see photocopiable sheet 134). If there are many teams, two or three teams could move from station

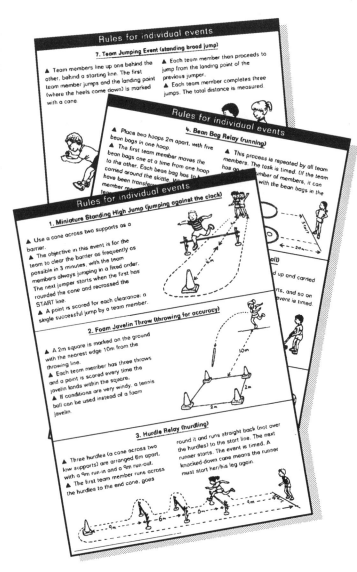

PHYSICAL EDUCATION

Outdoor and adventurous activities

Perhaps more than any other activities within the physical education curriculum, 'Outdoor and adventurous activities' provide meaningful opportunities for the personal and social development of children – not least because the situations that the children may experience can bring with them real consequences, such as the discomfort resulting from not packing a waterproof or forgetting to include a drink in your provisions when preparing for a long ramble. Of course, one pupil's difficulty may provide a practical opportunity for the rest of the group to exercise some thought for others – for example, through a willingness to share their own supplies with someone in need. It has been said that work in 'outdoor and adventurous activities' is essentially concerned with real life.

Any activity which is undertaken away from the school site is usually expensive in terms of both money and curriculum time. It will not be practical for the majority of schools to offer a complete outdoor and adventurous experience to children on this basis. Schools will thus need to maximise opportunities for outdoor and adventurous activities within the confines of their own grounds and buildings. A number of activities are offered in this chapter which seek to provide for this. Although the activities themselves do not take place in an outdoor environment, the children can still be challenged to exercise a range of skills required for safe and responsible conduct 'in the wild' through imaginative problem-solving situations.

Safety in outdoor/adventurous activities

The types of activity within the outdoor and adventurous activities programme of study, when offered in the immediate locality or the school grounds, will not usually be of a hazardous nature. However, it is important that safety principles are clearly understood by both the teacher and the pupils, in preparation for participation in traditional outdoor pursuits at a later stage (and for outdoor experiences in everyday life). Schools should consider and instigate an 'off-site' policy covering all activities away from the classroom and offering specific guidelines for adventurous activity, including risk assessment. Teachers will need, particularly when working off the school site, to be aware that:

▲ 'Loco parentis' cannot be set aside at any time until the pupils are returned to the care of their parents.

▲ The quality of group control depends upon experience and judgement. Teachers should always be familiar with the location of the activity and confident about the lesson content.

▲ Any equipment used should conform to recognised standards.

▲ Risk assessment should precede the activity. Teachers need to anticipate possible dangers involving particular environments: risks associated with climbing on walls, balancing on beams, the proximity of water and so on.

▲ Weather conditions can influence the activity, and should be taken into account at the planning stage as well as on the day of the event.

▲ Flexibility and sensitivity to the needs of the group often make the difference in determining whether the experience is a positive or negative one for the children.

▲ Responsible and appropriate behaviour should be expected of the class at all times. Remember that irresponsible behaviour by one pupil can be a threat to the safety of the whole group.

In summary, safe practice is dependent upon:-

▲ awareness of potential hazards;

▲ sound judgement about what constitutes a dangerous situation;

▲ adequate supervision.

Key stage progression

Outdoor and adventurous activities in the primary school are not immediately concerned with the traditional outdoor pursuits such as canoeing, sailing, mountaineering and rock climbing, though many children may experience these activities as part of school-organised visits to outdoor centres. A quick checklist for use in planning such a visit is given below, and may be photocopied. Much can be achieved in offering children an appropriate foundation in outdoor and adventurous activities within the school and the local environment. Indeed, for many schools, difficulties associated with timetabling, resources, finance and staff experience will make this approach necessary for delivering the programme of study for outdoor and adventurous activities.

Bearing in mind that outdoor and adventurous activities need to be taught at specific points rather than continuously through the key stage, the work could realistically include:

▲ basic orienteering exercises using the school grounds and possibly local parkland;

▲ problem-solving activities using indoor and outdoor school facilities;

▲ planned low-level walks.

Additionally, though this is not a requirement, it may be useful to include some basic campcraft (where expertise is available) in offering children a more complete 'survival' experience.

Outdoor and adventurous activity visits

This is a quick reference checklist when planning a visit.

1. What are the aims of the visit?

2. Has the consent of the head and governors been given? Have they been kept informed of further developments?

3. Will the site/facility/resources fully meet the aims of your visit?

4. Are the Centre staff's qualifications appropriate? (Seek advice from your LEA advisory service if unsure.)

5. Will you have a contract with the provider?

6. What insurance cover do you have?

7. Have you issued medical forms to pupils?

8. When will you make a preliminary visit?

9. What arrangements will you make for collecting money?

10. Have you informed parents and obtained their consent?

11. Have you arranged dates/times to meet parents, pupils (if necessary), staff and volunteers to discuss the visit?

12. Have you collated information about the visit to be kept in school?

13. Have school staff been briefed about emergency procedures?

14. Have you read the appropriate sections in *Safe Practice in Physical Education*, published by the British Association of Advisers and Lecturers in Physical Education? (Appendices 3 to 6 in particular give useful advice on medical/consent forms, letters to parents, codes of conduct and so on.)

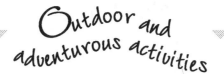

ORIENTEERING

To be introduced to basic orienteering in the school grounds. To develop an understanding of how maps can be used as an aid to route finding. To develop teamwork and co-operation skills, and build self-reliance through decision-making.

†† *Whole-class discussion; orienteering activity in groups of 4.*

🕐 *Introduction 15–20 minutes; outdoor/adventure activity 35–45 minutes.*

Previous skills/knowledge needed

The children will need to have the ability to interpret basic plans and maps, and be familiar with the idea of using simple signs and symbols on maps.

Key background information

This activity will help children to use a map or plan. Participants are required to find a series of 'stations' which are located in different places around an area of ground. It may be presented as a competitive activity, with speed of completion as the objective; but this is not necessary in the early stages of the activity. It provides a useful combination of vigorous activity, map-reading skills and teamwork.

Much of the knowledge required to sustain this activity will be developed through other areas of the curriculum, particularly geography. Orienteering can provide some useful reinforcement and consolidation of map-reading skills. The teacher should thus include work on orienteering close to planned units on map-reading in the classroom, where a map is interpreted as a symbolic picture of the ground.

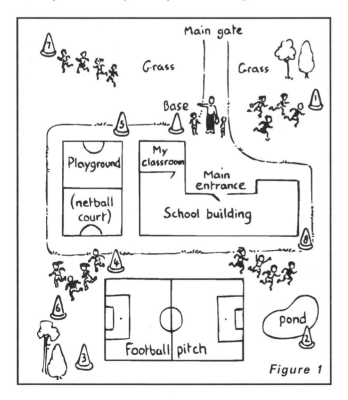

Figure 1

The following teaching points may be helpful.

▲ *Stay together as a group and work at the pace of your slowest team member.*

▲ *Make your decisions collectively. Appoint a team leader to sort out any disagreements. Decide who will carry the map, do the recording and so on.*

▲ *Do not set off too quickly – you may be running for a long time, and you will need to conserve your energy.*

▲ *Make the boundaries very clear, emphasising that no station is beyond them. On no account should any group stray out of bounds.*

Preparation

The teacher will need to provide at least one copy for each team of a plan/map of the school grounds, showing the significant features: grassed areas, trees, fences and so on. The map should be drawn to scale as far as possible, and should be laminated. An example is shown in Figure 1. Prior to the activity, the 'stations' (a letter, word or simple drawing on a small piece of coloured card in polythene can serve as a marker) will need to be deployed around the school grounds. Try to position these so that they are not too obvious. One copy per team (perhaps reduced onto a smaller card) of the score sheet (photocopiable sheet 138) should be made.

Resources needed

Brightly coloured card for making 'station' markers, small polythene bags (or a laminating machine), drawing pins or an industrial staple gun, laminated (or polythene-wrapped) map cards, pencils, stopwatches, small note-pads, one score sheet (copy of photocopiable sheet 138) per team.

What to do

Start in the classroom with a discussion about the objectives of the activity. The teams of four children have to locate the stations around the school grounds by using their maps. Each station is identified by its own code: a letter, word or drawing. Pupils need to record the station code in order to prove that a particular station has been visited. They should return to base after identifying each individual station. The team with the fastest time for completing the course wins. Points can also be awarded for each station correctly identified, in order to record each team's achievement.

Initially, the children should look for eight stations. To promote fair competition, it is helpful if each group negotiates the stations in a different order.

Suggestion(s) for extension

Once the children become familiar with the activity, the number of stations could be increased to 16. With appropriate supervision, it may be possible to set up a more demanding course in less familiar surroundings, such as the local park. By establishing the direction north, information about stations can be given using compass points and distances.

PHYSICAL
EDUCATION

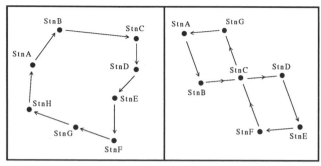

Figure 2

Initially, children will find it easier to return to a central base after locating each station. As their skills develop, they can attempt a circular or cross-over course (see Figure 2).

Suggestion(s) for support
For children lacking confidence, restrict the initial number of stations to three or four. They could use the classroom or hall as a first course to be negotiated.

Assessment opportunities
Observe how effectively the children co-operate in their teams. Can they establish a sense of direction? Are they capable of pacing their movement around the course? Do they record accurately and honestly? Do they persevere in finding the more difficult stations?

Reference to photocopiable sheet
Photocopiable sheet 138 is a score sheet or card on which each team can record the station codes and time taken to complete the course. If more than eight stations are used, a second score card will be needed.

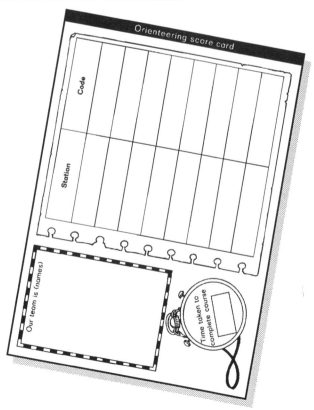

PROBLEM SOLVING

To work together in a group towards achieving a common goal. To undergo a series of 'adventure'-based problem-solving activities in order to develop their initiative and decision-making capability. To make imaginative use of the school grounds in creating an adventure environment.

†† *Whole-class introduction; groups of 4 for problem-solving activity; whole-class conclusion.*

🕐 *Introduction 15–20 minutes; outdoor/adventure activity 60 minutes (20 minutes per task); conclusion (discussion) 20 minutes.*

Previous skills/knowledge needed
The children will need the ability to work co-operatively in small groups.

Key background information
Using a variety of relatively inexpensive and accessible items such as planks, tyres and ropes, a number of physical challenges can be created for pupils to overcome when working in small groups. Initiative, clear thinking, leadership and co-operation will generally be needed by the children. A feeling of 'adventure' can be introduced through the adoption of an imaginative theme or storyline which links the tasks; the tasks themselves can also be used in isolation, depending upon the ability of the children.

The following teaching points may prove useful.
▲ *Don't rush into hasty decisions – think carefully about the consequences of your actions before proceeding.*
▲ *Involve everybody in the group in any decisions taken – make sure everyone has a say and is heard.*

Preparation
The teacher will need to reproduce a sufficient number of adventure task sheets: at least one set for each group (photocopiable sheets 139 to 141). The various activities will need to be set up beforehand in the school grounds.

Resources needed
Ropes of various lengths, balls of string, light planks, car tyres, hoops, blindfolds, skittles or plastic cones, photocopiable sheets 139, 140 and 141.

What to do
Organise the class into groups of four pupils. Distribute the adventure task sheets and explain the tasks. After some discussion, allocate groups to the various tasks. Each group should also be given two light planks (or one light plank) and a small car tyre which they will need to transport throughout their 'adventure'. With large classes, it will be necessary to duplicate the activities so that all the groups can remain occupied. Try to set up the tasks in such a way that it is

PHYSICAL EDUCATION

possible to keep all the groups in sight and under supervision.

Three tasks are set. 'Trust Walk' (photocopiable sheet 139) requires the child to feel their way along a length of string or rope while blindfolded and being guided by a 'sighted' group leader. The string should be attached to a series of fixed points (such as trees, shrubs, fences, poles and the ground). Obstacles to negotiate should be positioned at intervals around the course. A challenging obstacle course could even be set up in the school hall. This exercise is primarily concerned with establishing effective and reassuring communication between the leader and the group.

'Escape the Fire' (sheet 140) requires a hoop to be suspended from two trees or a set of goalposts. The hoop represents a tunnel through which the children have to move themselves and selected items of equipment. The hoop should be suspended securely, to prevent it twisting.

'Crossing the Poisonous Swamp' (sheet 141) involves the children manipulating two light planks and a tyre in order to cross a marked area without touching the ground. They must use the items of equipment to stand on.

Allow each group approximately 20 minutes on each activity, then reassemble the whole class for a debriefing session. Ask them:
▲ Which activity did you find the most difficult? Why?
▲ Did your group co-operate effectively?
▲ How did you negotiate the various obstacles?
▲ How did you get the planks through the tunnel?
▲ How did the tyre help you to cross the swamp?

Suggestion(s) for extension
The tasks can be made more difficult. In the 'Trust Walk', the course can be made more tortuous and can contain obstacles to climb over and balance along. In 'Escape the Fire', the 'tunnel' can be smaller or be suspended further from the ground, perhaps requiring children to pass the equipment through it. Smaller items for crossing on present a greater challenge in 'Crossing the Poisonous Swamp'.

As the children grow in confidence, the whole activity can be made competitive as a race against the clock. It may be possible to combine the tasks with an orienteering exercise, in which the children have to find the location of each challenge from maps and directions.

Suggestion(s) for support
For those children requiring a lesser challenge, the following variations may be helpful:
▲ Keep to straight lines, with few twists and turns, in the 'Trust Walk'.
▲ In 'Escape the Fire' simply suspend a low string (say 40cm from the ground) which might represent an electrified fence to negotiate, rather than the more difficult 'tunnel'.
▲ Use hoops, into which the children are allowed to step, rather than planks in 'Crossing the Poisonous Swamp'.

Assessment opportunities
These activities test mental agility and speed of social interaction more than physical agility. Observe how effectively the children arrive at decisions. Which children are prepared to take the lead? Do they support each other and respect each other's views? How well do they accept responsibility?

PHYSICAL EDUCATION

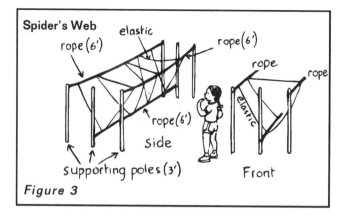

Figure 3

Reference to photocopiable sheets

Photocopiable sheets 139, 140 and 141 present the scenarios for the three problem-solving tasks. One copy of each sheet should be given to each group. The teacher will also find the sheets useful in setting up the equipment.

In the 'Crossing the Poisonous Swamp' task, the children can be allowed to assume that any of the items of equipment will support their weight on the swamp surface; but they should be sensible about keeping in balance.

THINKING ON YOUR FEET

To reinforce basic orienteering and problem-solving skills. To develop team co-operation skills further through competitive activity.

†† *Teams of 4 children.*

🕐 *This forms the basis of a half-day activity.*

Previous skills/knowledge needed

The pupils need to be able to work together in a small group, and to have basic experience of maps and map symbols.

Preparation

The teacher needs to set out the equipment for the three activities shown in Figures 3, 4 and 5 on the field or playground. A number of score sheets (or cards) will also be required (photocopiable sheet 142) to record the competing teams' performances. For the 'Map memory' task, the teacher needs to draw and photocopy four simple sketch maps depicting different areas of the school grounds.

Resources needed

Three strong ropes, each about 20m long (join some skipping ropes together), a ball of knicker elastic (available from a local millinery shop or haberdasher), six strong wooden poles, beanbags and table-tennis bats, copies of four sketch maps showing different areas of the school grounds, stopwatches, a score card (photocopiable sheet 142) for each team.

Key background information

This lesson combines orienteering and problem-solving skills. The following teaching points will be useful.

▲ *Although the activities are against the clock, try not to rush things. Make sure that you think things through carefully together before starting a particular activity.*

▲ *Make sure that everybody in your group has a say.*

What to do

Organise the class into teams of four. There are three activities to complete. Each team is timed over each activity, with the fastest team winning. The three activity times can then be totalled to produce an overall winner. Each team will have to record its times on the team score card.

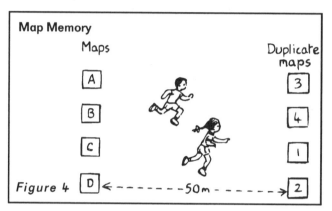

Figure 4

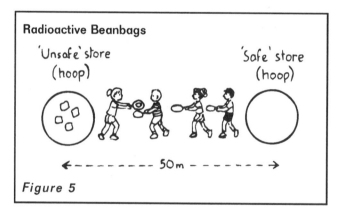

Figure 5

Spider's Web (see Figure 3)

This requires patience and agility. Set up a 3-D spider's web using poles, ropes and elastic. The children start at one end and have to move through to the other end without touching the web. If one of the team touches it, he/she has to start again. Timing starts as soon as the first child enters the web, and stops when all the team have come through.

Map Memory (see Figure 4)

This provides useful practice for orienteering. You need to have drawn four simple sketch maps depicting different areas of the school grounds, then duplicated them. Place the two identical sets about 50m apart. Assign letters to one set (A, B, C, D) and numbers to the other set (1, 2, 3, 4). The children are required to look at one map at a time and remember it, then run the 50m and select its duplicate from the other set. The activity is timed. If the children match two maps incorrectly, they must repeat that part of the task.

PHYSICAL EDUCATION

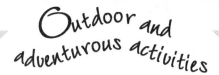
Radioactive Beanbags *(see Figure 5)*

In this problem-solving activity, the children have to find ways of transporting the four contaminated beanbags from an unsafe store (a hoop) to a safe store about 50m away (another hoop). The children must not touch the beanbags by hand, and can only use the bats to carry them. Close exposure to the bags through carrying them is limited to 3 seconds at a time, so the children will have to work out a relay procedure in order to avoid contamination.

Suggestion(s) for extension

Make the openings through the spider's web smaller. Present the children with increasingly complex and similar maps to match up. Substitute tennis balls for the beanbags to make transport more difficult.

Suggestion(s) for support

Make the web easier to negotiate. Use map symbols for matching, rather than a full sketch map. Increase the permitted exposure time in the radioactive beanbag activity.

Assessment opportunities

Observe how well the children work together. Do they listen to each other and communicate effectively (for example, discussing the activity before they start and sharing information during the activity)? Do they obey the rules? Do they record their team performances accurately?

Reference to photocopiable sheet

Photocopiable sheet 142 is a team score sheet or card which should be copied (perhaps onto card) and given to each team.

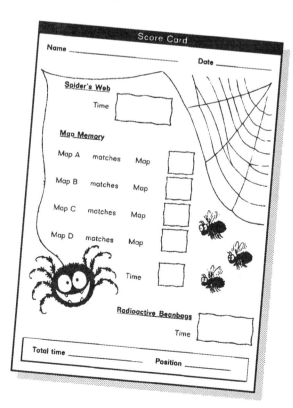

LOW-LEVEL WALK

To be introduced to basic expedition work. To develop the planning skills necessary for safe and responsible walking in the countryside.

†† *Whole-class discussion and planning; groups of 4 for walk; whole-class debriefing.*

🕐 *Discussion and planning in school 3–6 hours; whole day allocated to walk; debriefing (back in school) 2 hours.*

Previous skills/knowledge needed

The children will need the ability to make sense of a large-scale map using basic Ordnance Survey map symbols, together with an understanding of scale and direction.

Key background information

Low-level walks may take place in a variety of locations including woodland, coastline and open country. In addition to heightening their environmental awareness, much can be done to introduce the children to basic expedition planning involving route finding, safety, clothing, footwear and food provision. The children should be aware that planning a safe and manageable journey across unknown countryside needs careful thought and thorough preparation.

The teacher will, of course, need to be very familiar with the route selected, and the demands it makes of the children (both physical and intellectual) will have to be matched to their capabilities. However, the children should be given as much responsibility as possible when considering, among other things, the safety factors involved and the provisions and clothing required. Actual route planning and decisions relating to suitable rest stops should be a collaborative exercise between the teacher and the class.

The following teaching points will be useful.

▲ *Remember that the weather can change dramatically in the course of a day. Clothing should take account of this, without being too bulky or uncomfortable.*

▲ *Choice of food should be determined by its nutritional value and lightness – remember you will be carrying it for at least half the day.*

▲ *Rest stops are important. It is important to plan where, for instance, you will stop to eat.*

▲ *Always set off on time and always calculate what time you intend to arrive at your destination. This is known as your estimated time of arrival or ETA.*

▲ *Most importantly, you must agree to stick together and to travel at the speed of your slowest member.*

Preparation

The teacher will need to comply with school and/or LEA policy requirements governing offsite visits.

Having identified a suitable walk for the class – about 10 to 12 kilometres, preferably over undulating terrain, requiring about three hours' walking with appropriate stops – the

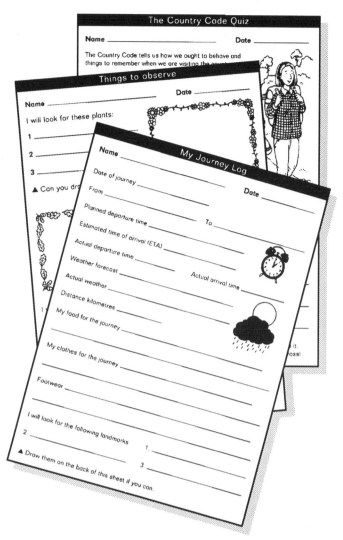

sheet 145; this will generate discussion about how we can keep the countryside clean and safe for ourselves and wildlife. (Some previous discussion may be necessary.)

Organise the class into groups of four and ask them to complete the sections of their journey log (sheets 143 and 144) which relate to planning and preparation. They should also make sketch maps based on the teacher's map.

During the walk

The children remain in their groups. Each group should be given the opportunity to lead some phase of the journey, using their sketch maps to identify landmarks and geographical features. Each group should also take its turn in bringing up the rear, making sure that no litter is left behind. The class must stay together and in view of adults.

After the walk

The children will need to evaluate the effectiveness of their planning and whether any unforeseen circumstances arose. Were their provisions appropriate, for instance; and did their footwear stand up to the journey? Did they arrive at their destination on time? What was the weather like? Was their group successful in leading the rest of the class when required to do so? The walk might also provide a stimulus for descriptive and creative writing, while features observed might assist ongoing work in science and geography.

Suggestion(s) for extension

It may be possible, with children who have appropriate experience, to work directly from a large-scale Ordnance Survey map rather than a simplified sketch map. The use of a compass and grid references as aids to navigation can also be introduced to provide greater challenge.

Suggestion(s) for support

Some children will require a very simple sketch map in order to make sense of their journey. Try to organise the groups to maximise the support available from the teacher and the other children. Ready-made sketch maps, to which the children are required to add one or two additional features during the walk, may also be helpful.

Assessment opportunities

Observe how well the children look after each other. Do they stick together when walking, encouraging their slowest members appropriately and moving at their pace? Do they remember and observe the Country Code? Are they able to keep going without having to rest too frequently?

Reference to photocopiable sheets

The journey log sheets (pages 143 and 144) allow the children both to plan various aspects of the journey and to record what they observe. They children can draw more plants, trees, animals and birds on the back of page 144.

The answers to the Country Code Quiz (photocopiable sheet 145) are shown above.

teacher will need to walk the proposed route in order to complete a risk assessment, identifying any potential hazards such as proximity to water, roads or steep slopes, and to establish points of interest and suitable places to rest. A large sketch map indicating north (or an Ordnance survey map with a scale of 1:25 000) will need to be prepared or obtained, and the route marked on it. This will stimulate useful discussion, with the children being made aware of the landmarks they need to look out for. The teacher will also need to duplicate a journey log (sheets 143 and 144) and a copy of the 'Country Code Quiz' (sheet 145) for each pupil.

Resources needed

Small pieces of card (for making sketch maps); coloured pens or crayons (for drawing and marking map symbols); photocopiable sheets 143, 144 and 145.

What to do

Before the walk

The children will need to understand that travelling in the countryside brings with it responsibilities associated with respect for the environment. In order to become familiar with the Country Code, the pupils should complete photocopiable

Swimming

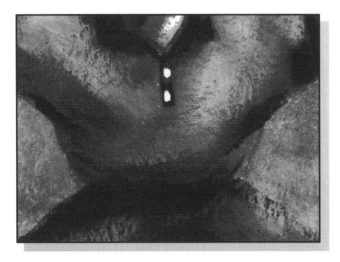

The provision of swimming teaching in Key Stage 2 varies considerably. For the majority of schools, the amount of swimming made available to pupils will depend on the policy adopted by the local education authority. LEA swimming programmes are usually supported by teams of professional swimming teachers, who give guidance to the teaching and provide for a safe learning environment. Many schools, however, depend on their own resources (particularly those schools who are fortunate in having their own swimming pool), and are sometimes able to plan their swimming programme in slightly more flexible ways. Clearly, because swimming is a potentially hazardous activity, it is necessary that anyone supervising swimming should have appropriate qualifications, particularly in life-saving and resuscitation. In addition to curriculum and lesson support material, much of this chapter is concerned with the necessary procedures and organisational arrangements necessary to ensure that children are taught under safe conditions.

The lesson materials presented assume that pupils will experience at least one year of weekly swimming lessons in Key Stage 2. This amount of time would seem to represent a realistic period in which to deliver the National Curriculum Programme of Study for swimming. Indeed, many authorities would advocate twice this amount in order to offer a meaningful swimming experience. Remember that the PoS in swimming goes beyond simply enabling pupils to swim with reasonable confidence: it also includes a requirement to address water safety and survival.

PHYSICAL
EDUCATION

The swimming lesson

It is necessary to differentiate classes for swimming according to ability, both for reasons of safety – it would be dangerous, for instance, to attempt to teach beginners in deep water – and to allow more effective progress to be made throughout the class, since the appropriate activities for a beginner will be very different from those for an advanced swimmer.

As in any classroom subject, the children will display a range of aptitude in swimming, thus demanding an initial assessment to determine their exact capabilities. The majority of children will improve steadily as their swimming experience grows. In the course of a two-year swimming programme, it is not unusual for beginners to end up as advanced performers. For some children, however, progress is less marked. Children who are fearful of water, for instance, may make relatively few gains until their confidence develops; sometimes this represents a long and difficult process.

The structure in which the sample lesson plans in this chapter are presented – three lessons for beginners, three for improvers, then three for advanced swimmers – does not represent a model of continuous progression for any one child over a two-year swimming programme; but it does more genuinely reflect (in a somewhat artificial form) the organisational requirements for the teaching of swimming. You should thus use the material presented in a flexible way, rearranging the lessons to suit the beginners, improvers and advanced swimmers you are teaching concurrently.

The photocopiable sheets are designed to assist you with the technical aspects of the basic swimming strokes and survival techniques. Copies may also be laminated and used on the poolside by pupils who are able to work more independently. They could also be displayed in the classroom.

Strictly speaking, it is possible to teach the PoS for swimming in Key Stage 1. However, so many practical difficulties arise that KS1 swimming is rarely viable.

Skill demands in swimming

Swimming is an activity in which the pupil has to combine a number of different actions in a co-ordinated and fluent manner – with the added, unique performance requirement of breathing at predetermined times (though many children embark on their first few strokes while holding their breath).

Swimming technique in KS2 might be said to include four main considerations: arm action, leg action, body position and breathing. Although the recognised swimming strokes represent complex actions, it is relatively easy to isolate one particular component of the overall action – the leg kick, for example – and provide opportunities for the learner to practise and consolidate it in a focused way. Such an action can be practised on its own (often with the help of floats or other buoyancy aids) and then, when sufficiently well-mastered, be combined with the other components in the full stroke.

Since any activity undertaken in water proceeds at a slower pace than a similar activity undertaken on dry land, it is easier for the teacher to provide useful guidance during the activity. Thus the learner is often able to correct or modify a faulty action more effectively, and to receive more immediate reinforcement of sound technique, than in other areas of PE.

The lesson plans in this chapter are samples and do not attempt to cover in detail the teaching of every stroke (except in the photocopiable sheets); however, this should be achieved over the Key Stage, with specialist support as needed.

Safety in swimming

Teachers should establish the following safe procedures.
Arrival and departure
▲ Children should always enter and leave the swimming pool area under supervision, and be counted into and out of the swimming pool area.
In the changing rooms
▲ Encourage good behaviour in the changing rooms, as this will set the tone of the lesson.
▲ For the safety of the individual and the group, it is strongly recommended that no jewellery of any kind be worn in the water. Provision will need to be made for the safe keeping of valuables. It may be necessary to discuss this with children who wear jewellery for religious purposes, or who wear Medi-alert bracelets or similar items (see note on page xx).
▲ Remind the children to attend to their personal toilet requirements and to be clean before entering the pool.
Teacher responsibilities
Teachers need to:
▲ wear suitable clothing and appropriate footwear;
▲ make sure that the children are aware of the deep and shallow ends of the pool;
▲ know the location and function of safety equipment – the telephone, resuscitation apparatus and first-aid box;
▲ check the condition of the buoyancy aids for safety;
▲ be able to contact pool staff immediately in the event of any emergency.
Emergency drill
▲ This will need to be clearly understood by all children, and should be practised. They should be taught how to attract the teacher by shouting or waving.
▲ Teachers will need to carry a whistle at all times, to be used strictly as a safety aid and **not as a teaching aid**. Special arrangements will need to be made for hearing-impaired children.
▲ The recommended emergency drill procedure is:
1. ONE long blast on the whistle means STOP! The children should stand or tread water and face the teacher.
2. TWO long blasts on the whistle means the children should LEAVE THE WATER by the shortest route and stand well away from the edge of the pool.
Pool organisation
▲ The teacher should count the number of children prior to entry into the water and on leaving the water.

▲ The class register should be available on the poolside, and should clearly identify children who may be at risk in a water environment (for example, children with epilepsy or diabetes) or who have skin complaints such as eczema which could be affected by chlorinated water.

Lesson organisation

▲ Children should be familiar with routine procedure when entering the pool area – for example, they should know exactly where to stand, sit or line up. **NB** No child should be allowed to enter the water until told to do so.

▲ The swimming ability of the children should be assessed at the beginning of a unit of work, and records should be kept of the progress of individual pupils.

▲ The teacher will need to adopt a position on the poolside such that all pupils in her or his care are constantly visible.

▲ There are many advantages an arrangement such that the children work in pairs. It encourages co-operation and confidence, assists in class management and provides an additional safety check, with the children adopting some responsibility for their partners' well-being.

Key Stage progression

Swimming in Key Stage 2 will need to include:

1. **Knowledge of the emergency procedure** for school lessons. **NB** Procedures to be followed in the event of an emergency at the pool outside school lessons (or an emergency in other contexts, such as a visit to a beach) should also be understood by the children.

2. **Development of stroke technique**
▲ Back crawl.
▲ Front crawl.
▲ Breast stroke.
▲ Butterfly stroke (advanced swimmers only).
To include breathing, timing and body position, with a view to producing a competent swimmer after two years.

3. **Development of stamina**
▲ Timed swim – try to increase the distances (number of lengths or widths) completed in a set time by pupils over a period of weeks.

▲ Set distance – try to reduce the time taken by pupils to swim a set distance.

▲ Increase workrate over a set distance and explore the changes in pulse rate and breathing (slowfastslow).

4. **Familiarisation with a range of games**
▲ Relay games involving taught skills, such as surface dives, sculling, picking up sinkers and swimming through hoops.

▲ Water polo and water volleyball, involving skill practices and game situations.
▲ Ball tag.
▲ Sharks and minnows.
▲ Pearl divers.
▲ Simon says.
(See lesson plans for rules of these games.) Many more aquatic games are suitable at this level.

5. **Establishing water confidence**
▲ Sculling: feet first, head first, change of body shape (in various combinations of).
▲ Rotation: forwards, backwards and laterally.
▲ Jumping in: body shape in the air.
▲ Shallow dives (depending on the suitability of the pool).
▲ Underwater swimming: through hoops or a set distance.
▲ Floating: body shapes leading to sequences.
▲ Picking up sinkers.
▲ Surface dives: head first, feet first.
▲ Push and glide: front and back.
▲ Starts and turns.

6. **The knowledge and practice of water safety**
▲ Recognising a casualty involving a:
• non-swimmer;
• weak swimmer;
• injured swimmer.
▲ Recognising an unconscious person in the water.
▲ Rescues based on the poolside: reaching with poles, clothes and so on; throwing ropes and buoyant objects. Children should know the safety points, how to give instructions and reassurance to the casualty and how to give simple aftercare.

▲ Initiative situations using learned skills: making appropriate responses to a mock-emergency situation.
▲ Making assessments of situations.
▲ Emergency drill.
▲ Outdoor water safety:
• safety in the countryside, for example at reservoirs, lakes, canals, gravel pits, rivers;
• safety at the seaside;
• dangers of ice;
• dangers and safe practice of water sports such as fishing, canoeing, sailing and windsurfing.

7. **Knowledge and practice of survival in water**
▲ Effects of cold on the body.
▲ Swimming in clothes with a buoyant object.
▲ Treading water in conditions which present varying degrees of difficulty.
▲ H.E.L.P. position (Heat Escape Lessening Posture).
▲ Huddling together to conserve heat.
▲ Shallow entry (head to remain above water).
▲ Safe exit from water.
▲ Evaluation of survival skills.

8. **Hygiene and pool safety and regulations**
▲ Whistle drill.
▲ Pool emergency procedure.
▲ Routine for changing, to include hygiene.
▲ Do's and don'ts.

9. **The physiology of survival**
▲ How the body loses heat.
▲ How to prevent heat loss.
▲ Effects of cold on the body.
▲ Hypothermia.

BEGINNERS – TERM 1

To be able to make a safe entry and exit into/out of water. To develop confidence in the water.

†† *Group of 4–10 pupils, split into groups of 3 for part of the activity.*

🕐 *Warm-up 5 minutes; skill development 20 minutes; conclusion 5 minutes.*

Previous skills/knowledge needed

The class should understand the procedures for changing, hygiene routine, safety rules and whistle drill.

Preparation

The teacher will need to ensure that the necessary equipment, such as floats and buoyancy aids, is stored safely at the poolside.

Resources needed

Inflatable arm bands (as required), three inflatable rubber balls, a shallow pool area, floats (if needed).

Key background information

The following teaching points will be useful.

Safe entry

Tell the children to:

▲ Sit down on the pool edge to start.

▲ Place both hands together on the pool edge, next to your hips. [If the poolside is crowded, specify placing hands to either left or right.]

▲ Twist around.

▲ Lower your body into the water.

▲ Stand and wait for further instructions.

Safe exit

▲ Place both hands on the side of the pool.

▲ Push down.

▲ Put one knee on the poolside.

▲ Climb out.

▲ Move away from the poolside.

Walking in shallow water

▲ Walk across the width of the pool, close to the side, at a pace that is comfortable.

▲ Use your arms for balance.

▲ Don't take strides that are too big.

▲ Remember, it is not a race! Keep in step with the person in front of you.

Ball tag

▲ Walk at all times!

What to do

Start by reminding the children about the safety and whistle drill and then distribute armbands as necessary. This will need to be determined by questioning the children about their confidence and observing their capabilities when in the water.

Warm-up activity

Space the group around the edge of the pool and practise entries and exits on command with the children working in pairs – one observing, the other working.

Skill development

Line the group up one behind the other in the water, holding waists. Ask the children to walk next to the wall around the edge of the pool.

Now divide the group into two and repeat, with each group walking in a 'Z' formation through the pool (see Figure 1).

Now organise the group into 'waves' of three. The children must start on the poolside, demonstrate a safe entry, walk through the pool, demonstrate a safe exit, and reform their lines away from the edge of the pool on the other side (see Figure 2).

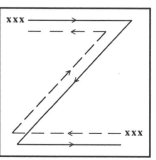 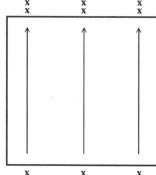

Figure 1   Figure 2

Conclusion

Conclude with a game of 'ball tag' in shallow water. The children can move anywhere in the shallow area, by walking or swimming. Three children are 'on' and have a ball each. They must try to touch another child with the ball; this child then takes the place of her/his catcher (**NB** the ball cannot be thrown). The new child 'on' cannot 'tag' her or his particular catcher.

At the end of the session, make sure that the children leave the pool in a safe and orderly manner and line up on the poolside.

PHYSICAL EDUCATION

Suggestion(s) for extension

More able children could practise walking in a line without holding the person in front. Ask them to speed up the walking pace or reverse the direction of the walking line.

Suggestion(s) for support

Be prepared to give as much verbal encouragement as is necessary.

Encourage the children to touch the side of the pool when walking. Offer additional pairs of armbands for those children who lack confidence.

Assessment opportunities

Observe whether the children can enter the water safely. Can they walk unaided through the pool? Can they leave the water safely?

BEGINNERS – TERM 3

To continue building water confidence through jumping into the water and picking up objects from the pool floor and to learn the back crawl leg kick.

†† *Groups of 3–10 pupils.*

🕐 *Warm-up 5 minutes; skill development 20 minutes; conclusion 5 minutes.*

Previous skills/knowledge needed

The children should have prior experience of being submerged (see previous activity). They will need to be confident about floating on their fronts and backs.

Preparation

The teacher will need to ensure that there are sufficient armbands, buoyancy aids and 'sinkers' (objects that do not float, such as rubber bricks) for the group. Copies of photocopiable sheet 150 can be laminated for use at the poolside by the teacher and/or the children.

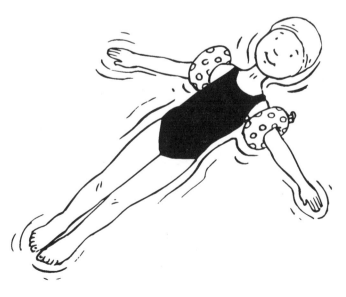

Resources needed

Inflatable armbands and buoyancy aids (floats) as needed, sinkers, a shallow area (1m depth) of the pool, copies of photocopiable sheet 150 (as required).

Key background information

The following teaching points will be useful.

Picking up 'sinkers'

▲ Drop the sinker carefully near your feet.

▲ Keep your feet on the floor.

▲ Take a deep breath, bend knees and submerge your head.

▲ Pick up the sinker.

▲ Stand up.

Floating

▲ Relax on your back and keep your body stretched.

▲ Rest your head on the water.

▲ Keep your legs together.

▲ Keep your feet relaxed, but stretch them forward.

Jumping in

▲ Toes at the edge.

▲ Small space between your feet.

▲ Bend your knees and jump feet first into the water.

▲ Spread your arms wide for balance.

▲ Bend your knees on landing.

What to do

Warm-up activity

Distribute pairs of armbands as necessary. Then space the group out in the water. Ask the children to work in pairs (as this provides time and, if necessary, assistance for appropriate recovery of breath), taking turns to drop and pick up the sinker.

Skill development

Ask the children to hold a float across their chests and practise pushing and floating on their backs, returning to a standing position each time. Now ask the children to push

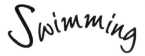

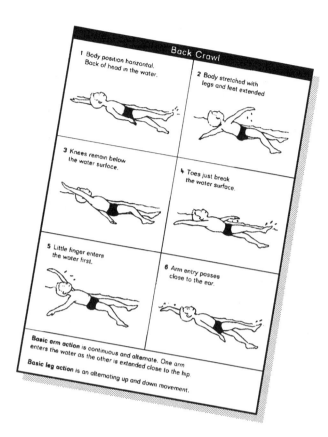

Back Crawl

1 Body position horizontal. Back of head in the water.

2 Body stretched with legs and feet extended

3 Knees remain below the water surface.

4 Toes just break the water surface.

5 Little finger enters the water first.

6 Arm entry passes close to the ear.

Basic arm action is continuous and alternate. One arm enters the water as the other is extended close to the hip.

Basic leg action is an alternating up and down movement.

and float on their backs, but to kick with their legs as in the back crawl (see photocopiable sheet 150).

Now repeat the above without floats. Provide opportunities for each child to work individually. This will assist your observation and subsequent guidance.

Conclusion

Arrange the group spaced out around the edge of the pool. Ask them to jump in, one at a time.

Suggestion(s) for extension

More able children could try working without armbands; or try making a 10m swim without stopping, propelled by back crawl leg kicks; or add arm pulls (see photocopiable sheet 150) to the leg kicks.

Suggestion(s) for support

Less confident children could continue with the use of floats, and use extra armbands if necessary.

Assessment opportunities

Observe whether the children can submerge their heads. Can they perform a back crawl leg kick wearing armbands? Without armbands? With or without a float?

Reference to photocopiable sheet

Photocopiable sheet 150 shows the movements for back crawl, including the leg kick used in this activity. Laminated copies could be kept at the poolside for reference, or displayed in the classroom. These photocopiables are chiefly a teacher resource, but children may find them useful.

BEGINNERS – TERM 6

To learn the breast stroke (full stroke). To practise underwater swimming.

ᵢᵢ *Group of 4–10 pupils.*

🕐 *Warm-up 5 minutes; skill development 20 minutes; conclusion 5 minutes.*

Previous skills/knowledge needed

The children will need to have some prior experience of submerging. They should have practised breast stroke technique in water (standing or crouching).

Preparation

The teacher will need to ensure that armbands, floats and hoops are available on the poolside. Laminated copies of photocopiable sheets 146 and 149 can be provided.

Resources needed

Inflatable armbands and floats (as needed), hoops for swimming through, photocopiable sheets 146 and 149, a shallow pool area.

Key background information

The following teaching points will be useful.

Breast stroke leg kick

▲ Heels up to bottom, feet turned out.

▲ Push back with heels.

▲ Keep your legs in the water.

▲ Try to move your legs symmetrically and simultaneously.

▲ Keep your legs behind your hips at all times.

Breast stroke arm action

▲ Keep your hands in view at all times.

▲ Press your hands sideways, downwards and backwards, at an angle of about 45 degrees to the water surface.

▲ Recover smoothly, bringing your hands together at the chin. Make a slight pause.

▲ Push your arms straight out together. Repeat the stroke.

Swimming

Timing
▲ The sequence of the stroke is PULL, BREATHE, KICK, GLIDE.
▲ As the arms push forward, the legs drive back vigorously.

What to do
Warm-up activity
Distribute armbands as necessary. Spread the group in the water space (the shallow area). Ask the group to practise the mushroom float and the star float.

Skill development
Ask the children to practise pushing and gliding on their fronts as far as possible, with floats. Then ask them to add the breast stroke leg kick to this action. (See photocopiable sheet 149).

The floats can now be put on the poolside and the group asked to practise the breast stroke arm action while walking across the pool with their faces out of the water. They should move their arms through the water, and pause after each pull with arms extended. Finally, they should try the whole stroke over a 10m distance.

Conclusion
Conclude the activity by challenging the children to swim underwater through a suspended hoop. This is a useful task to conclude a breast stroke lesson, since a strong breast stroke arm action (at a higher angle than usual) will help the child to become submerged.

Suggestion(s) for extension
Children who are confident in floating could try moving from the mushroom float to the frontal star float without breathing in between. More able swimmers could extend the slide between strokes; in the final activity, they could approach the hoop with a swim, dive through it and continue swimming.

Suggestion(s) for support
Children who find the swimming activity difficult could use additional armbands, and practise the leg kick with a float.

Assessment opportunities
Observe whether the children can float with confidence. Can they swim 10 metres using the breast stroke? Can they submerge themselves and swim through the hoop?

Reference to photocopiable sheets
Photocopiable sheet 146 shows the actions for the mushroom float and star float; photocopiable sheet 149 shows the actions for the breast stroke.

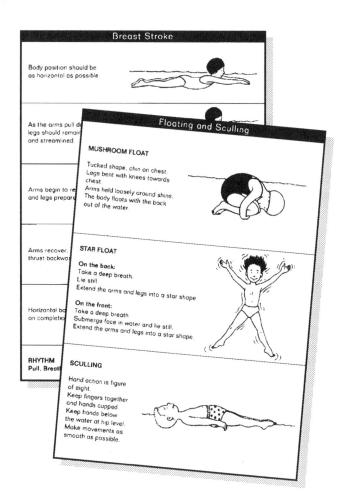

Breast Stroke
Body position should be as horizontal as possible.

As the arms pull down, legs should remain and streamlined.

Arms begin to recover and legs prepare.

Arms recover, thrust backward.

Horizontal body on completion.

RHYTHM
Pull, Breathe.

Floating and Sculling

MUSHROOM FLOAT
Tucked shape, chin on chest.
Legs bent with knees towards chest.
Arms held loosely around shins.
The body floats with the back out of the water.

STAR FLOAT
On the back:
Take a deep breath.
Lie still.
Extend the arms and legs into a star shape.

On the front:
Take a deep breath.
Submerge face in water and lie still.
Extend the arms and legs into a star shape.

SCULLING
Hand action is figure of eight.
Keep fingers together and hands cupped.
Keep hands below the water at hip level.
Make movements as smooth as possible.

IMPROVERS – TERM 1

To learn push and glide techniques on the back. To complete a 10m swim on the back, using legs for propulsion.

†† *Groups of four to twelve pupils, split into groups of four for skill development.*

⏱ *Warm-up 5 minutes; skill development 20 minutes; conclusion 5 minutes.*

Previous skills/knowledge needed
The children should have experience of floating on their backs and swimming on their backs without buoyancy aids.

Preparation
The teacher will need to ensure that a sufficient number of floats (or other buoyancy aids) is available on the poolside – one per pupil). Copies of photocopiable sheets 146 and 150

will be needed to assist the teacher in improving children's stroke technique. These could also be enlarged and displayed on the poolside or in the classroom.

Resources needed
One float per child, a standing depth area of the pool, photocopiable sheets 146 and 150.

Key background information
The following teaching points will be useful.
Mushroom float
▲ Take a deep breath.
▲ Bring your knees to your chin, then tuck. (See photocopiable sheet 146.)
▲ Hold your knees.
▲ Keep as still as you can and float, for as long as possible. Exhale into water.
Star float
1. Back
▲ Take a deep breath and exhale slowly while floating.
▲ Lie still on the water.
▲ Extend your arms and legs into a star shape.
2. Front
▲ Breathe deeply and hold it, then exhale.
▲ Lie still on your front with your face in the water.
▲ Extend your arms and legs into a star shape. Lift head to breathe.
Push and glide on the back
▲ Put your hands on the wall, keeping them level. (Hold rail if there is one.)
▲ Place your feet on the wall, together and close to your hands.
▲ Lean back so that your body is along the surface of the water and your arms are straight.

▲ Push away from the wall with your legs, extend your body but keep your arms by your side.
Back crawl leg kick
▲ Extend your legs and swing from the hips, kicking with alternate legs.
▲ Feet relaxed but stretched forward.
▲ Keep your legs close together.
▲ Ankles loose and floppy, knees below the water.
▲ Small splash with your toes.
Sculling
▲ Keep your body flat and still on the surface of the water, facing upwards.
▲ Lead with your head.
▲ Make small arm movements level with your hips. (See photocopiable sheet 146.)

What to do
Remind pupils about the whistle drill and safety rules.
Warm-up activity
Spread the group out and practise the three types of floating: mushroom; star on back; star on front. (See photocopiable sheet 146).

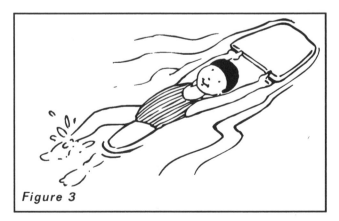

Figure 3

PHYSICAL EDUCATION

Skill development

Now work across the pool (standing depth of water) in groups of four. Ask each group to float on their backs with floats held to their chests. Introduce the back crawl leg kick. (See photocopiable sheet 150.) Without floats, practise the push and glide on the back. Now ask the group to combine the push and glide with the back crawl leg kick for whatever distance they can. Stagger the starts so that each child works individually.

Conclusion

Conclude by asking the children to scull head first across the pool.

Suggestion(s) for extension

More confident children could try moving from a mushroom float to a star float (front) without taking an intermediate breath and without standing up. They could hold the float in front of their heads when performing the back crawl leg kick (see Figure 3). They could try the push and glide on the back with the arms extended behind the head.

Suggestion(s) for support

Continue with floats, or use additional buoyancy aids, if necessary.

Assessment opportunities

Observe whether the children can push and glide without the use of buoyancy aids. Can they swim 10m on their backs using the back crawl leg kick?

Reference to photocopiable sheets

Photocopiable sheets 146 and 150 show the actions for the mushroom and star floats, sculling and the back crawl leg kick. They can be copied for the teacher's use; or enlarged and laminated for pupil use at the poolside or display in the classroom.

IMPROVERS – TERM 3

To understand the dangers associated with cold water immersion. To develop the skills necessary to survive cold water immersion.

†† *Group of 4–12 pupils.*

🕐 *Warm-up 10 minutes; skill development 15 minutes; conclusion 5 minutes.*

⚠ *Make sure that children do not spend too long in wet clothes, either in or out of the water.*

Previous skills/knowledge needed

Pupils should have a basic understanding of how the human body reacts in a cold environment by protecting its core temperature, and how hypothermia can arise.

Preparation

The teacher should ensure that floats or other buoyancy aids are available on the poolside. The children will need to bring some old clothing – shirts, blouses, trousers, skirts – suitable for use in water. Photocopiable sheet 147, illustrating the H.E.L.P. position, will be useful for the children as well as the teacher.

Resources needed

Floats, old clothing (see above), photocopiable sheet 147, a standing depth area of the pool.

Key background information

Hypothermia occurs after continued exposure to cool temperatures, even as mild as 16°C (60°F). Hypothermia is a dangerous lowering of the body temperature that requires emergency treatment. It can be fatal.

The H.E.L.P. (Heat Escape Lessening Posture) position assists the body in retaining heat in cold water by minimising heat loss through convection (and energy loss through body movement). It is achieved by using a floating aid as follows:
▲ lying still and floating back at an angle of approximately 45 degrees;
▲ keeping legs together and slightly bent;
▲ keeping arms bent on the chest, holding the floating aid;
▲ keeping the head clear of the water.

What to do

Discuss situations in which the children might have to enter water or swim when dressed. Stress that in such situations, they should kick off their shoes or boots.

Warm-up activity

In standing depth water with pupils wearing trousers/skirt and shirt/blouse over their swimming costume, ask them to practise:
▲ safe entries and exits;
▲ walking forwards, backwards, sideways (to right and left);
▲ walking with changes of direction to avoid others.

Skill development

Still wearing clothes, and using floats, the children should practise treading water and swimming on their fronts, faces clear of the water. They should experiment with different kinds of leg kick.

Now ask individual children, using their floats, to: demonstrate a safe entry; tread water for 30 seconds; swim 15m on the front with the face clear of the water; and make a safe exit.

Next, the children should practise the H.E.L.P. position wearing clothes, keeping still for as long as possible.

Conclusion

To conclude, ask the children to remove their outer clothing and swim at least two lengths of the pool in normal swimwear, with their own choice of stroke.

Suggestion(s) for extension

Children who are confident in the situations above could try swimming in clothes, and practising the H.E.L.P. position, in deep water.

Suggestion(s) for support

For children who are less confident, wearing only one item of outer clothing may help, since there will be less weight (drag) in the water and less obstruction to free movement than if they are fully clothed.

Assessment opportunities

Observe whether the children can effect safe entries and exits when clothed. Can they demonstrate the H.E.L.P. position effectively?

Reference to photocopiable sheet

Photocopiable sheet 147 shows the H.E.L.P. position for conserving heat when immersed in cold water. This is a teacher resource, but laminated copies could be used by children at the poolside or displayed in the classroom, perhaps in relation to topic work on Water, Sailing or Survival.

IMPROVERS – TERM 6

To demonstrate a confident swim over 50m using front crawl, breast stroke and back crawl.

†† *Group of 4–12 pupils; pairs for conclusion.*

🕑 *Warm-up 5 minutes; skill development 15 minutes; conclusion 10 minutes.*

Previous skills/knowledge needed

Pupils will need to have learned and practised the front crawl, breast stroke and back crawl, and to have experience of floating in various shapes.

Preparation

The teacher may find it useful to have photocopiable sheets 148, 149 and 150 available for reference.

Resources needed

A swimming area about 7m by 25m, of variable depth, photocopiable sheets 148, 149 and 150.

Key background information

Teachers will need to emphasise the technical aspects of the three strokes to the group (see photocopiable sheets 148, 149 and 150 for details). Each pupil should be given

PHYSICAL EDUCATION

Swimming

the opportunity for sustained practice with minimal interruption; this is best achieved by the teacher feeding in technical guidance to the children while they are swimming, without making them stop and start again.

What to do
Warm-up activity
Space the group out in standing depth water. Revise floating. Ask the children to devise their own floating sequence, making different body shapes on both the front and the back and moving from one shape to the other without standing up in between.

Skill development
The children should now work down the length of the pool, swimming first 50m back crawl, then 50m front crawl, then 50m breast stroke. (See the appropriate photocopiable instruction sheets for technical details.) They should then repeat the exercise.

Conclusion
Working with a partner in standing depth water, the children should produce a floating sequence using mirroring, movement towards, movement away from, movement side by side and so on. Each pair's sequence should be performed for the rest of the group. This creative work provides the basis for synchronised swimming, which the children may explore in later work.

Suggestion(s) for extension
A group of confident swimmers could make a group floating sequence. Confident individuals could extend the distance of their swim from 50m to 100m.

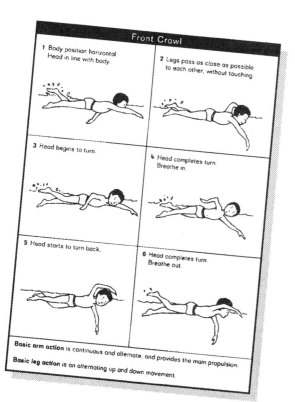

Suggestion(s) for support
Shorten the distance of the swim for less confident swimmers. If necessary, provide more guidance for the floating sequence, limiting the child to simply copying the movements of her/his partner.

Assessment opportunities
Observe whether the children complete the swim and demonstrate sound technique. Can the children devise a water sequence and perform it effectively?

Reference to photocopiable sheets
The photocopiable instructions sheets 148, 149 and 150 show the actions for front crawl, breast stroke and back crawl respectively. (Front crawl is not covered already in these sample lesson plans, but comes within the Key Stage progression.) The teacher should use these sheets for reference, but demonstrate the strokes directly to the children.

ADVANCED – TERM 1

To learn the push and glide technique, on the back with arms extended. To swim 10m using back crawl (arms and legs).

†† *Group of 4–12 pupils; skill development in groups of 4.*

⏲ *Warm-up 5 minutes; skill development 20 minutes; conclusion 5 minutes.*

Previous skills/knowledge needed
The children should have experience of floating on their backs. They should already have practised the back crawl leg kick technique.

Preparation
The teacher will need to ensure that sufficient floats (or other buoyancy aids) are available on the poolside. Photocopiable sheet 150 will be useful as a teacher resource.

Ask each group to push and glide on their backs with arms extended sideways, not using floats. Then they should pull their arms down to their sides for propulsion combining this action with the back crawl leg kick. Gradually, they should modify the arm movements to back crawl technique and practise the full stroke.

Conclusion

Conclude with the whole group sculling both head first and feet first.

Suggestion(s) for extension

More able swimmers could attempt log rolls of 360 degrees. They could extend the distance of the glide; and bend arms at the beginning of the glide, pulling the body to the wall (which helps to develop a more powerful and rapid 'push' action). Stronger swimmers could also try the single arm pulls without buoyancy aids.

Suggestion(s) for support

Less able swimmers could use the buoyancy aids for longer periods, either to practise the early stages of the activity or to attempt the whole activity.

Assessment opportunities

Observe whether the children can push and glide on their backs with extended arms. Can they swim 10m with the complete back crawl stroke?

Reference to photocopiable sheet

Photocopiable sheet 150, showing the actions for the back crawl stroke (sometimes called 'backstroke'), will be useful to the teacher in guiding pupils through the correct sequence of movements.

Resources needed

One float per child, photocopiable sheet 150, the deep-water area of the pool.

Key background information

The following teaching points will be useful.

Log roll (lateral roll)

(This is a useful warm-up activity, since it develops agility in the water.)

▲ Keep your body fully extended, arms stretched out beyond your head.

▲ Use your arms to roll your body over sideways in the water, through 180 degrees.

Back crawl arm action

▲ Work your arms alternately.

▲ Extend your arm when you lift out of the water.

▲ Turn your arm so that your little finger re-enters the water first (see photocopiable sheet 150).

▲ Pull down sideways with a bent arm, to the hip.

What to do

Recap on whistle drill and safety procedures. This activity should be carried out in the deep water area of the pool.

Warm-up activity

Spread the class out and practice log rolls, front to back and back to front.

Skill development

The children should work in groups of four, swimming across the pool. Without buoyancy aids, they should practise the push and glide technique with arms extended beyond the head. Now ask each group to combine a glide with a back crawl leg kick.

Next, ask them to hold a float against the chest with the right arm and practise the back crawl leg kick with left arm pulls; then to repeat using right arm pulls.

PHYSICAL EDUCATION

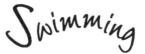

ADVANCED – TERM 3

To develop a fuller understanding of cold water survival in terms of energy conservation. To learn further skills to assist cold water survival.

†† *Groups of 4–12 pupils.*

🕐 *Warm-up 5 minutes; skill development 20 minutes; conclusion 5 minutes.*

⚠ *Make sure that children do not spend too long in wet clothes, either in the pool or out of it.*

Previous skills/knowledge needed
The children should understand the effects and causes of hypothermia. (A brief account is given on page 93; any book on life saving, outdoor pursuits or water safety will offer a fuller explanation.) They should have previous experience of water survival techniques such as treading water and the H.E.L.P. position.

Preparation
The teacher will need to ensure that a range of different buoyancy aids are available on the poolside: life-jacket, plastic bottles, life-rings and a variety of floating objects. The children will need to bring some old clothes suitable for use in water: trousers/skirts and shirts/blouses.

Resources needed
A range of buoyancy aids, photocopiable sheet 147, the deep-water area of the pool.

Key background information
The teacher will need to emphasise the importance of conserving energy in cold water. This is necessary both to retain body heat (which will be carried away by convection currents in the water) and to delay exhaustion if action (such as swimming) is needed.

The following teaching points are appropriate to the 'huddle'.

▲ Huddle together to retain body heat (see photocopiable sheet 147).

▲ Hold each other's waist/shoulder, NOT the neck (which may interfere with breathing).

▲ Knees either bent up or straight.

▲ Maintain the balance of the group huddle.

▲ Try to move as little as possible.

What to do
Warm-up activity
Ask the group, when they are wearing clothes, to practise making a safe entry into deep water and a safe exit from it.
Skill development
Ask the group to practise swimming on their fronts with their faces clear of the water, using the breast stroke leg kick while holding onto (or wearing) a float. They should practise

this with a range of different buoyancy aids such as plastic bottles, life-rings and life-jackets (anything that retains air will act as a float and so assist buoyancy). This helps the children to realise that a range of everyday objects can be used in this way.

Next, they should make a safe entry; swim 15m on their fronts with their faces clear of the water, using the breast stroke leg kick; then make a safe exit.

By this time, they will appreciate the need to conserve energy. They should demonstrate the H.E.L.P. position and then the group huddle.
Conclusion
Finally, the group should remove their outer clothing and swim 100m with their own (individual) choice of stroke.

Suggestion(s) for extension
Extend the time for which the H.E.L.P. position and the huddle are maintained.

Suggestion(s) for support
Restrict the use of buoyancy aids to polystyrene floats, which give greater buoyancy than 'improvised' versions such as plastic bottles. Children could swim in only one item of outer clothing; or they could work in a standing depth of water.

Assessment opportunities
Observe whether the children can effect a safe entry and exit. Can they swim 15m with a buoyancy aid and then exit safely? Can they make and sustain an effective huddle?

Reference to photocopiable sheet
Photocopiable sheet 147 shows the H.E.L.P. position (Heat Escape Lessening Posture) and the 'huddle'. It should be used by the teacher for reference; copies could also be laminated for use by children at the poolside or for display in the classroom, perhaps in relation to topic work on Heat or Energy.

ADVANCED – TERM 6

***To show good style in the swimming of front crawl,
back crawl, breast stroke and butterfly.***

†† *Groups of 4–12 pupils; conclusion in groups of 4.*

🕐 *Warm-up 5 minutes; skill development 15 minutes;
conclusion 10 minutes.*

Previous skills/knowledge needed

Pupils will need to have experienced floating and rotation (the
log roll). They should display reasonable confidence in using
the four strokes, and be able to work productively in groups.

Preparation

The teacher will need photocopiable sheets 148, 149, 150
and 151 for reference.

Resources needed

A swimming pool area of approximately 7m by 25m, of
variable depth, photocopiable sheets 148 to 151.

Key background information

The teacher will need to re-emphasise the technical points
associated with each stroke (see the relevant photocopiable
sheets). Try to keep the group working all the time: when they
are swimming the four strokes, make sure that they do not
rest or wait unnecessarily (but allow resting where needed).

What to do

Warm-up activity

Spread the group out in deep water. Revise floating – face
up, face down, facing sideways – and changing body shape.
Ask the children to combine floating and rotation to make a

sequence, moving from one position to the next without
standing up.

Skill development

Ask the children to swim up and down the length of the
pool: 25m butterfly; 100m (four lengths) back crawl; 100m
front crawl; 100m breast stroke. The emphasis should be
on good technique rather than speed.

Conclusion

Organise the children into groups of four and ask them to
devise a group sequence involving rotation and floating. This
activity is a simple form of synchronised swimming.

Suggestion(s) for extension

Time the 100m swims and establish individual target times
for improvement.

Suggestion(s) for support

Shorten the distance of the swims.

Assessment opportunities

Observe whether the children demonstrate good style in the
four strokes. Can each group plan, perform and evaluate
effectively in making its water sequence?

Reference to photocopiable sheets

Photocopiable sheets 148 to 151 show the actions for the
four strokes required of children at Key Stage 2. They are
intended primarily for teacher use; but copies could be
laminated for use by children at the poolside or for display in
the classroom.

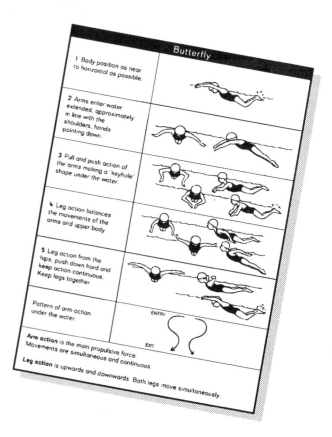

**PHYSICAL
EDUCATION**

Assessment and record-keeping

Assessment in physical education needs to fulfil a number of important functions:

▲ to support pupil learning by informing the teacher about individual pupils' strengths and weaknesses;

▲ to inform the pupils themselves about their progress and achievements;

▲ to provide the teacher with information about the effectiveness of lesson material.

Where assessment is effective, it will motivate pupils; help teachers to plan better lessons; help to establish curriculum continuity; and provide essential information for recording and reporting purposes.

Assessment in physical education brings with it a number of unique features:

▲ The hall, playground and field represent very different working areas from the classroom – for example, children are often widely dispersed.

▲ Learning outcomes are not usually expressed in written form, but in movement and action.

▲ Health and safety obligations require constant vigilance by the teacher, who needs to watch over the whole class at all times.

Bearing these contextual features in mind, assessment should be *meaningful* and *manageable*. It must always be remembered that physical education is a practical subject. In order to fulfil the functions listed above, there should be no need to generate a vast amount of documentation: the system of assessment can be memorised.

PHYSICAL
EDUCATION

Formative and summative assessment

Assessment in physical education is a necessary process for establishing and communicating the achievement of pupils. What constitutes a manageable assessment system?

Clearly, it would prove an impossible task to make fine judgements about all aspects of a child's involvement and progress through the physical education curriculum. However, throughout any particular lesson, the teacher will constantly be evaluating how individual children and groups of children cope with the work presented to them. The 'Assessment opportunities' sections in the sample lessons provided throughout this book suggest the type of **observations** that teachers might make in order to inform their understanding of pupil progress and learning. These observations help teachers to plan future work effectively, and the process is sometimes called 'formative' assessment. Some teachers find that they have to make some written record of pupil progress through a particular unit of work at fairly regular intervals in order to sustain their teaching. Other teachers are confident in their ability to remember their observations and to use this knowledge to inform the next stage of their teaching. It should be emphasised that there is no right or wrong way, and teachers will know their own strengths and weaknesses better than anyone else.

There will come a time, however, when all teachers need to make a permanent record of pupil achievement. This is usually required at the end of each school year in the form of a 'summative' assessment of pupil progress. Additionally, in England and Wales, a summative assessment at the end of each Key Stage is required by the National Curriculum. However, because physical education consists of a number of different activities (perhaps as many as seven or eight over one year), it is recommended that teachers record achievement at the end of each completed unit of work. Thus, if a unit of dance is completed in the autumn term (for instance), it would make more sense to record progress at the time the unit finishes than to wait until the end of the summer term.

The basis of summative assessment is an overall profile based on a portfolio or collection of evidence; it is not a series of 'snapshot' assessments made at different times. Records of achievement in PE will be necessary to compile the evidence for summative assessment, since children's written work is a minor part of their work in this subject area.

Provided that the school has established a progressive whole scheme of work for physical education, with concise

PHYSICAL EDUCATION

(Name) Steve Vermont

GOLD
merit award for

Outstanding effort with forward roll

(Personal Effort)

in
GYMNASTICS (PE)

Mr J. Simmons Class 5S teacher

Signed *Jarvis Simmons*

Figure 1

and clearly defined learning outcomes (not too many!) for each unit of work, then the class recording sheet for a given year provided on photocopiable page 152 should suffice and ultimately inform the end of Key Stage assessment in line with the End of Key Stage Description in the National Curriculum. (A key to the class recording sheet is provided on photocopiable page 153.)

It is recommended that a three-tier system of assessment, indicating three levels of achievement, is used for each activity and area of development:

▲ working below expectations (denoted by 1);
▲ working in line with expectations (denoted by 2);
▲ working beyond expectations (denoted by 3).

One advantage of this system is that it enables the teacher to determine at a glance the achievement profile of the class and that of each individual pupil across the full range of physical education activities.

Merit cards in PE

Completion of achievement profiles can be further assisted by awarding 'merit cards' at regular intervals to children who work well and/or try hard in physical education. Some examples are offered on photocopiable sheets 156 and 157, to help the teacher create a bank of suitable merit cards. A 'merit card' (bronze, silver or gold) may be activity-specific, as in 'Navigational Skill in O/A Activity' or 'Throwing in Athletics'; or related to personal effort, as in 'Perseverance', 'Working with Others' or 'Careful Handling of Apparatus'. However, the availability of awards for personal effort should ensure that the most unfit, non-sporty child could still get a merit, for 'Perseverance' in athletics, for example, even if he or she always came last.

PHYSICAL EDUCATION

National Curriculum
Physical Education Key Stage 2   Year Group _5_   Class _Mrs. Smith_

Please indicate the types of activity you have covered
with your class/year group under the headings below.

Term	Gymnastics	Dance	Games	Athletics	Outdoor and adventurous activity	Swimming
Spring '97	Theme: balance. • Linking three balances to make a floor sequence. • Balances on large apparatus. • Revision of forward roll. (10 lessons)	No dance this term. (autumn term)	Theme: invasion. • Control of ball using feet. • Small-side games (4 v 2) with emphasis on finding space. (8 lessons)	• Introduction to hurdling over single barrier. (2 lessons)	No O/A this term. (Summer term)	• Stroke improvement (all abilities). • Survival awards (more able).

Figure 2

Suitable 'merit award' categories for performance in PE could include the categories listed on photocopiable sheet 153 under the six types of physical education activity (categories a to p). Suitable 'merit award' categories for personal effort in PE could include:

▲ working with others;
▲ perseverance;
▲ outstanding effort;
▲ careful handling of apparatus.

The merit card itself can be added to by the teacher in the space provided (see example in Figure 1). For example, if a pupil works hard in gymnastics to perform a good forward roll, then this action might be added to the card so that this particular achievement can be recognised.

The teacher will need to keep a 'PE box' in the classroom into which all the individual merit cards are placed. The box can be emptied at appropriate intervals – say once per term – and the range of achievement shared and celebrated with the class.

Merit cards might also be used to inform parents about good progress, the children being allowed to take them home. They should also be kept for inclusion in individual records of achievement.

For the record

In order to guarantee curriculum coverage and continuity further, it is important that information briefly detailing the content of lessons be passed on from year to year. Photocopiable page 154 provides an appropriate pro forma for this purpose. Figure 2 shows an example of how this sheet might be filled in.

Finally, it is important that teachers themselves carry out some form of evaluation of the success of their own teaching. Photocopiable page 155 should provide some assistance in this process and provoke some useful reflection on the actual delivery of the Physical Education Programme of Study. It might usefully contribute to an audit of the Physical Education curriculum throughout the school; alternatively, it could be used by individual teachers two or three times a year to inform their own planning.

Teacher self-evaluation sheet

Criteria for evaluating the physical education lesson

1. Did the lesson(s) improve skill levels throughout the class?

2. Were the activities presented appropriate for all pupils?

3. Were the activities demanding enough to enhance previous fitness levels?

4. Were the teaching styles employed effective in promoting pupil learning?

5. What opportunities were provided to develop responsibility and initiative among pupils?

6. How much attention was paid to safe practice and the establishment of a safe working environment?

PHYSICAL EDUCATION

Photocopiables

The pages in this section can be photocopied for use in the classroom or school which has purchased this book, and do not need to be declared in any return in respect of any photocopying licence.

They comprise a varied selection of both pupil and teacher resources, including pupil worksheets, teacher resource material (such as technical instruction cards) and record sheets to be completed by the teacher or children. Most of the photocopiable pages are related to one or more individual activities within a particular chapter of the book; the relevant chapter is indicated at the top of the sheet, together with page references indicating where the lesson plans can be found.

Individual pages are discussed in detail within each lesson plan, accompanied by ideas for adaptation where appropriate – of course, the use of any sheet can be adapted to suit your own needs and those of your class. Sheets can also be coloured, laminated, mounted on to card, enlarged and so on where appropriate.

Pupil worksheets and record sheets have spaces provided for children's names and for noting the date on which each sheet was used. This means that, if so required, they can be included easily within any pupil assessment portfolio. Photocopiable sheets 152 to 157 are related to more long-term assessment and record-keeping processes discussed in the last chapter.

PHYSICAL EDUCATION

My Exercise Diary

Name _____   Date _____

Day	What did I do?	How long did it take?
MON		
TUE		
WED		
THUR		
FRI		

Weekly total _____

Which activity did I do the most? _____

Will it help my:

Stamina? _____

Strength? _____

Suppleness? _____

Heart and body

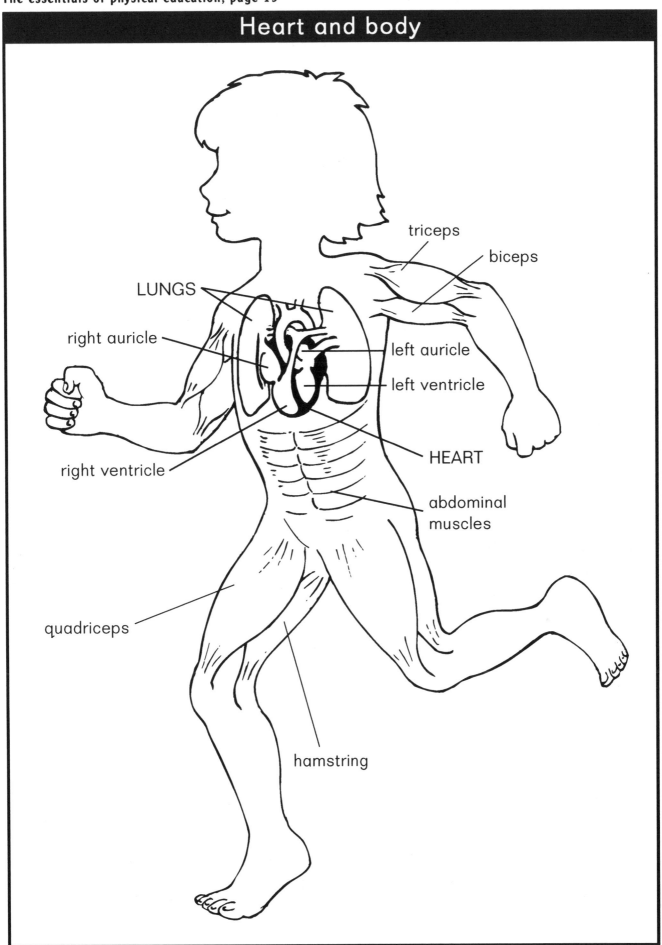

triceps

biceps

LUNGS

right auricle

left auricle

left ventricle

right ventricle

HEART

abdominal muscles

quadriceps

hamstring

Exercise and my body

Name _____   Date _____

▲ What happens when I exercise? (✓orX)

☐ I feel cold.   ☐ I get fat.
☐ I sweat.   ☐ I get taller.
☐ I feel hot.   ☐ My heart beats faster.
☐ I feel tired.   ☐ I go red.

To keep going you need STAMINA.

▲ Which parts of your body help stamina?

lungs   heart   muscles   eyes   feet   teeth

▲ Which exercise will give you more stamina?

running   swimming   jumping   diving

▲ How many times do you need to exercise to improve stamina?

☐ every day   ☐ once per week
☐ once per month   ☐ 3 times per week

PHYSICAL
EDUCATION

Exercise and my body

Name _____ **Date** _____

To lift, carry, push or pull yourself and objects you need to be STRONG.

▲ Which parts of your body help you to be strong?

head   heart   muscles   ears

If you are good at bending and stretching, you are SUPPLE.

▲ Which parts of your body help you to be supple?

joints   bones   muscles   veins

▲ What will make you more supple?

stretching   walking   eating   running

PHYSICAL
EDUCATION

The essentials of physical education, page 22

How does exercise affect my body?

Name _____   **Date** _____

Now you have tried three different kinds of exercise, here is a sheet for you to complete.

Can you name some ways in which your body changes during exercise?

Exercise makes your body work harder. Regular exercise will improve your fitness and health. You will be able to do more physical work without becoming tired.

STAMINA helps to keep you going. It means having enough energy to carry out prolonged activity in a comfortable way, without getting too tired or out of breath.

▲ Which parts of your body affect your stamina?
▲ What kind of exercise do you need to do to improve your stamina?
▲ How often do you need to exercise to improve your stamina?

STRENGTH is important for the everyday tasks of lifting, carrying, pulling and pushing your body or an object.

▲ Which parts of your body affect your strength?
▲ Why do you think some people are stronger than others?

SUPPLENESS *helps you move freely without sprains or strains.*

▲ Which parts of your body affect your suppleness?
▲ How can you become more supple?

Games activity card 1

1. Roll a ball around your waist.

2. Roll a ball around all the other parts of your body.

3. Use your hands to take the ball around your body, but do not let it touch your body.

Games, pages 27 and 30

Games activity card 2

4. Throw a ball (small or large)
high in the air.
Clap.
Let the ball bounce.
Catch it.

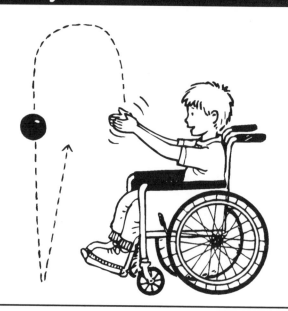

5. Throw a ball high.
Catch it with both hands.

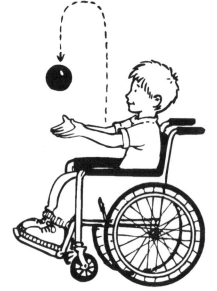

6. Throw a ball high.
Clap.
Catch the ball
with both hands.

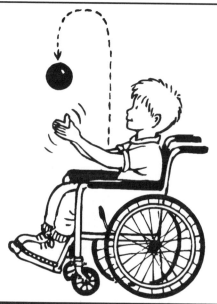

**PHYSICAL
EDUCATION**

Games activity card 3

7. Roll the ball against the wall.
Capture it with your hands.

8. Kick a ball against the wall.
Capture it with your foot.

**PHYSICAL
EDUCATION**

Games activity card 4

9. Send the ball (small or large) to your partner using hands or feet. Capture it when returned using hands or feet.

10. Bounce the ball to your partner. Catch on return.

11. Roll the ball away. Chase it. Capture it with your hands or feet or hockey stick.

PHYSICAL EDUCATION

Games, pages 32, 34 and 36

Games activity card 5

12. Keep a ball in the air using a bat for as long as you can.

13. Bounce a ball with a bat against the ground for as long as you can.

14. Stand three strides away from your partner.

How many hits can you make to each other:
▲ with one bounce per hit?
▲ with no bounces?

Games, page 37

Potted sports

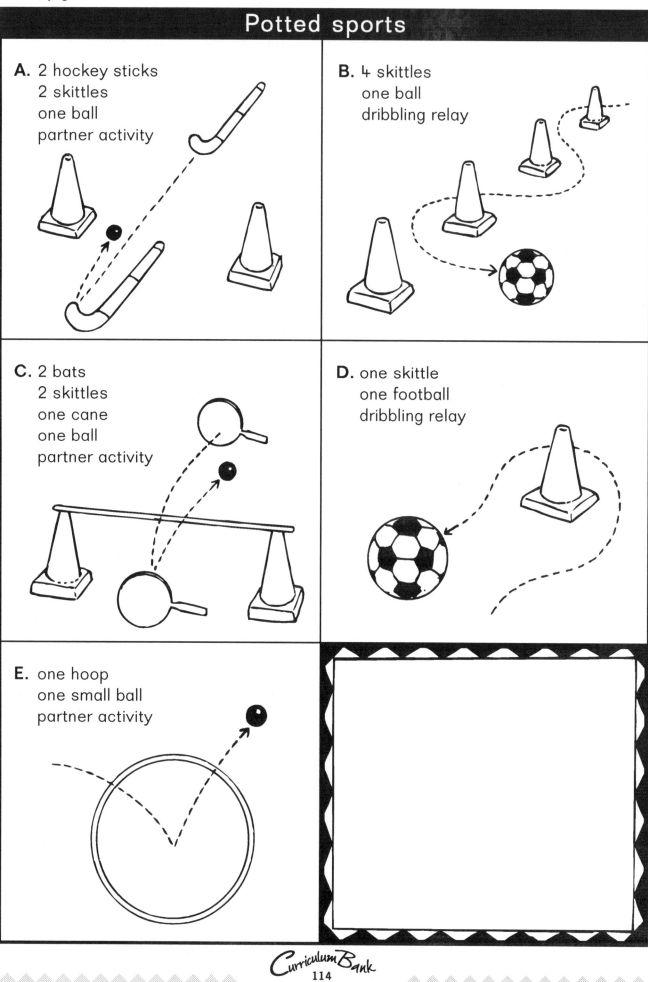

A. 2 hockey sticks
2 skittles
one ball
partner activity

B. 4 skittles
one ball
dribbling relay

C. 2 bats
2 skittles
one cane
one ball
partner activity

D. one skittle
one football
dribbling relay

E. one hoop
one small ball
partner activity

PHYSICAL
EDUCATION

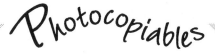
Pin Roll and Dish Roll

Pin roll

Lie on your back,
arms stretched beyond your head.
Make a long thin stretched shape.
Keep your fingers together and toes pointed.

As slowly as you can, roll sideways like a log until you are on your back again.
Maintain the same stretched shape until you have completed the action.

Dish roll

Lie on your back,
arms stretched beyond your head.
Make a long thin extended shape:
fingers stretched,
toes pointed.

Lift fingers and toes 10 cm off the ground.
Slowly roll sideways,
keeping your hands and toes off the
ground.
Maintain the extended shape.

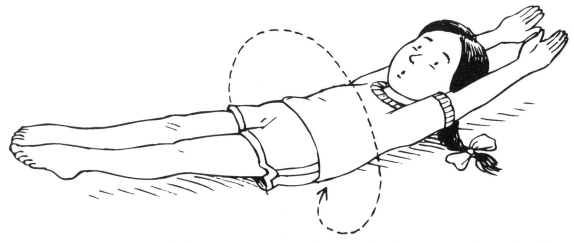

Maintain the same extended shape until you have rolled over onto your back again.

Egg Roll and Shoulder Stand

EGG ROLL

Kneel down, ankles close together.
Keep your toes pointed.
Stretch up high with your arms.

Now curl up and roll
slowly to one side.
Keep your body tightly
tucked up in a round shape,
with your knees and chin
kept close to your chest.

When you have completed your roll and are back on your knees,
stretch out again into your starting position.

SHOULDER STAND

Lie on your back on the floor,
hands by your sides, palms down;
legs close together, toes pointed.
Slowly curl your knees up to your forehead.
Lift your hips off the ground.

Slowly straighten your legs
towards the ceiling.
Point your toes.
Hold for three seconds.

Slowly lower your knees back
down towards your forehead.
Slowly uncurl, lowering your
hips to the floor.
Straighten your legs.
Point your toes to finish.

PHYSICAL EDUCATION

Gymnastics, pages 42, 45 and 46

Gymnastics warm-up bank

To start the lesson:
▲ Run, jump and stretch high OR
▲ Skip around the hall with a high knee action OR
▲ Demonstrate a variety of travelling actions using feet –
hopping, skipping, running, changing direction and speed.

Then move on to one or two of the activities listed below:

▲ On the spot stretch up high, then slowly curl
up tight on the floor.

▲ Start lying stretched out on your back, then
push into low bridge or bridge ('crab') position.

▲ Lie on your front and gently push your chest
high, keeping the fronts of your legs on the floor.

▲ Adapt a front support position with feet apart.
Keep your legs as straight as possible and walk
your hands back towards your feet, so that you
finish standing.

▲ Lie on your front. Raise your hands and your
feet off the ground. Can you roll over on to your
back without your hands and feet touching the
floor?

▲ Raise your hands above your head. Can you
sit down slowly on the floor with your hands above
your head? Can you stand up again with your
hands kept high in the air?

▲ Circle arms slowly forwards; then backwards.
Can you circle one arm forwards and the other
backwards?

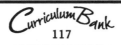

**PHYSICAL
EDUCATION**

Gymnastics, page 43

The Arabesque

Start in a long
stretched shape,
fingers close
together.

Balance on one foot
while maintaining the same
long stretched shape.
Extend the other leg
backwards and reach
forwards with your arms.

Try to make a 'T'
shape with your body.
Keep your chin up.
Hold this position for
3 seconds.

Slowly return to your starting position.

PHYSICAL EDUCATION

Gymnastics, page 43

Activities to encourage extension

Start with your arms by your side:
chin up,
tummy tucked in,
bottom tucked in,
legs straight,
feet close together.
Pretend that someone is pulling you
up towards the ceiling by your hair.

As slowly as you can,
take your arms out to
the side at shoulder height,
fingers together.

Bring your arms
together in front of you.
Keep them at shoulder height.

Bring your arms slowly up.
Keep your arms straight.
Stretch into a long thin shape.
Go up on to your toes. Hold for 3 seconds.
Come down onto your feet.
Slowly return to the starting position.

PHYSICAL
EDUCATION

Sequence development card 1

Starting Position	Action 1	Action 2	Finishing Position
Stand up on your toes as tall as you can. **Reach up.** **Stretch** your fingertips.	**Balance** on one foot.	**Roll** in a long, stretched shape.	**Stand up** on your toes as tall as you can. **Reach up.** **Stretch** your fingertips.
Stand up on your toes as tall as you can. **Reach up.** **Stretch** your fingertips.	**Balance** on one foot.	**Roll** in a long, stretched shape.	**Stand up** on your toes as tall as you can. **Reach up.** **Stretch** your fingertips.
Stand up on your toes as tall as you can. **Reach up.** **Stretch** your fingertips.	**Balance** on one foot.	**Roll** in a long, stretched shape.	**Stand up** on your toes as tall as you can. **Reach up.** **Stretch** your fingertips.

PHYSICAL
EDUCATION

Sequence development card 2

Starting Position	Action 1	Action 2	Finishing Position
Stand up on your toes as tall as you can. **Reach up.** **Stretch** your fingertips.	**Select a roll.**	**Select a balance.**	**Stand up** on your toes as tall as you can. **Reach up.** **Stretch** your fingertips.
Stand up on your toes as tall as you can. **Reach up.** **Stretch** your fingertips.	**Select a roll.**	**Select a balance.**	**Stand up** on your toes as tall as you can. **Reach up.** **Stretch** your fingertips.
Stand up on your toes as tall as you can. **Reach up.** **Stretch** your fingertips.	**Select a roll.**	**Select a balance.**	**Stand up** on your toes as tall as you can. **Reach up.** **Stretch** your fingertips.

PHYSICAL
EDUCATION

Sequence development card 3

Starting Position	Action 1	Action 2	Action 3	Finishing Position
Stand up on your toes as tall as you can. **Reach up.** **Stretch** your fingertips.	**Select a balance** on one body part.	**Roll** in a round shape.	**Select one action** of your own.	**Stand up** on your toes as tall as you can. **Reach up.** **Stretch** your fingertips.
Starting Position	**Action 1**	**Action 2**	**Action 3**	**Finishing Position**
Stand up on your toes as tall as you can. **Reach up.** **Stretch** your fingertips.	**Select a balance** on one body part.	**Roll** in a round shape.	**Select one action** of your own.	**Stand up** on your toes as tall as you can. **Reach up.** **Stretch** your fingertips.
Starting Position	**Action 1**	**Action 2**	**Action 3**	**Finishing Position**
Stand up on your toes as tall as you can. **Reach up.** **Stretch** your fingertips.	**Select a balance** on one body part.	**Roll** in a round shape.	**Select one action** of your own.	**Stand up** on your toes as tall as you can. **Reach up.** **Stretch** your fingertips.

PHYSICAL EDUCATION

Gymnastics, pages 46 and 48

Sequence development card 4

Starting Position	Action 1	Action 2	Action 3	Finishing Position
Select a starting position close to the floor.	**Balance** on one foot.	**Roll** in a round shape.	**Select one action** of your own.	**Select a wide** finishing position.
Select a starting position close to the floor.	**Balance** on one foot.	**Roll** in a round shape.	**Select one action** of your own.	**Select a wide** finishing position.
Select a starting position close to the floor.	**Balance** on one foot.	**Roll** in a round shape.	**Select one action** of your own.	**Select a wide** finishing position.

Gymnastics, pages 46 and 48

Sequence development card 5

Starting Position	Action 1	Action 2	Actions 3 and 4	Finishing Position
Select a starting position.	**Select** a jump.	**Select** a roll.	**Select two actions** of your own.	**Select** a finishing position.
Starting Position	**Action 1**	**Action 2**	**Actions 3 and 4**	**Finishing Position**
Select a starting position.	**Select** a jump.	**Select** a roll.	**Select two actions** of your own.	**Select** a finishing position.
Starting Position	**Action 1**	**Action 2**	**Actions 3 and 4**	**Finishing Position**
Select a starting position.	**Select** a jump.	**Select** a roll.	**Select two actions** of your own.	**Select** a finishing position.

PHYSICAL EDUCATION

Gymnastics, pages 48 and 49

Kicking Donkeys 1

Start in a squat position, arms out in front of you.

Place your hands on the floor in front of your body: hands shoulder-width apart, arms locked straight, **chin up.**

Take your weight onto your hands, lifting hips, **chin up**.

Kick your heels up to touch your bottom.

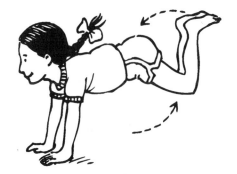

Quietly return to your starting position.

PHYSICAL EDUCATION

Gymnastics, pages 48 and 49

Kicking Donkeys 2

Start in a long stretched shape.

Lower your arms to
the floor in front of you.
Push one leg straight
out behind you.
Place your hands on the
floor in front of your body:
hands shoulder-width apart,
arms locked straight,
chin up.

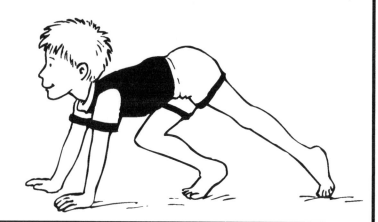

Take your weight
onto your hands,
chin up.
Kick your back leg
(straight leg) up
towards the ceiling.
Keep your front leg bent.

Your front leg lands gently
on the ground first.
Return to starting position.

PHYSICAL
EDUCATION

Gymnastics, page 49

Turns – quarter, half, full

1. Start in a long stretched shape, fingers together.

2. Swing both arms backwards.
Bend your knees.
Take off from both feet and stretch.

3. Turn 90° in the air, so that you land at a right angle to your starting position (¼ **turn**).

4. Turn 180° in the air, so that you land in the opposite direction from your starting position (½ **turn**).

5. Turn 360° in the air, so that you land back in your starting position (**full turn**).

PHYSICAL EDUCATION

King Cotton

See how the link flies out over the moorland,
See how the smoke in the valley clings,
See how the slate roofs shine in the drizzle;
This is the valley where Cotton is King.

See how the houses cling to the hillside,
Hear how the streets of children sing,
Wake to the scream of the factory hooter:
This is the valley where Cotton is King.

See how the hunger has eaten the faces,
Tired flesh to the bones just clings,
Dust in the lungs and the bodies are twisted:
This is the valley where Cotton is King.

Sleep is washed from the broken faces,
Morning clogs on the cobbles ring,
Off to the mill the weavers hurry:
This is the valley where Cotton is King.

You work all day to the loom's hard rhythm,
Scrabble and toil till your tired bones sing,
Then you crawl back home as the gas lights flicker:
This is the valley where Cotton is King.

This the land where children labour,
Where Life and Death mean the selfsame thing,
Where the many must work that few might prosper:
This is the valley where Cotton is King.

by Mike Harding
from *A Bomber's Moon* (Michael Joseph, 1987)

PHYSICAL
EDUCATION

Dance, page 60

Step patterns

Chorus
Each pair takes four steps towards the other – on the fourth beat they clap hands with the person opposite, then return (8 counts). Repeat.

Each pair passes round the other and returns (8 counts). Repeat.

The four make a right-hand star (8 counts), then make a left-hand star (8 counts).

Each pair takes four steps towards the other – on the fourth beat they clap one hand with the person opposite, then return (8 counts). Repeat.

PHYSICAL EDUCATION

Dance, page 60

More patterns

Two-handed (crossed)
turn – 8 turns to the
left and 8 to the right.

Hold hands and turn –
8 turns to the left and
8 to the right.

Promenade with partner
– turn on 8 and return.

Skip/sidestep to the left
(count of 4 and return).
Then skip/sidestep to
the right (count of 4
and return).

Skip, weaving in and out of
space following your partner
(count of 16 or 32).

PHYSICAL
EDUCATION

Athletics, pages 68, 69, 71, 72 and 74

My Athletic Record

Name _____   Date _____

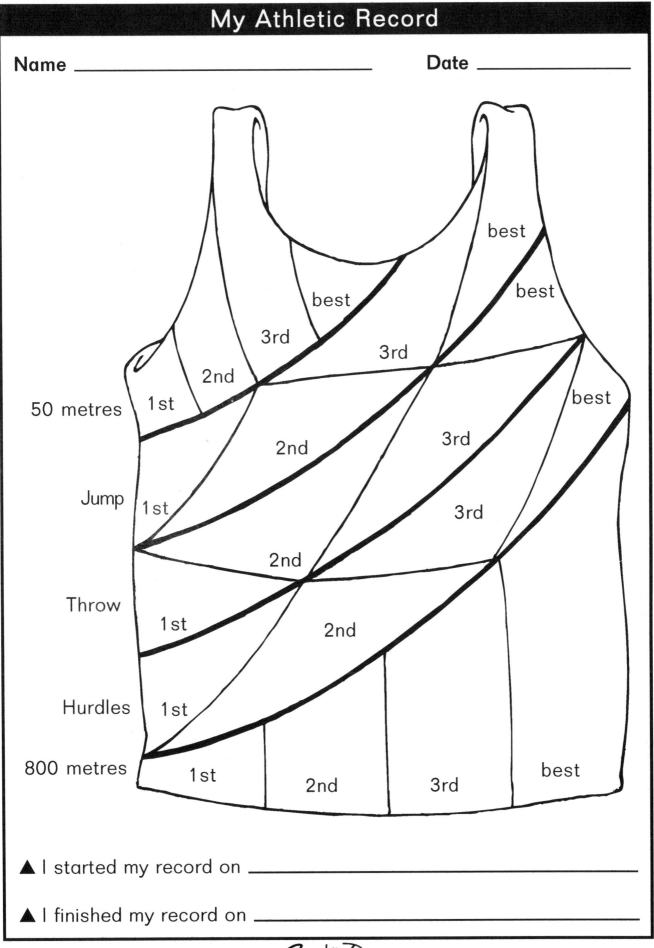

best

best

best

3rd

3rd

best

2nd

3rd

50 metres   1st

2nd   3rd

best

Jump   1st

3rd

2nd

Throw   1st   2nd

Hurdles   1st

800 metres   1st   2nd   3rd   best

▲ I started my record on _____

▲ I finished my record on _____

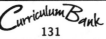
PHYSICAL EDUCATION

Event Record Sheet

Judge's name _____

Event _____

Team _____

Performance (time or distance recorded)

Position _____

1234567890123456789012345678901234567890123456789012345678901234567890

Points awarded

Long Jump

Athletics, page 75

Master Score Sheet

Event \ Team	1 Standing High Jump Perfor-mance	Score	2 Foam Javelin Throw Perfor-mance	Score	3 Hurdles Perfor-mance	Score	4 Bean Bag Relay Perfor-mance	Score	5 Slalom Relay Perfor-mance	Score	6 Team Throw Perfor-mance	Score	7 Team Jump Perfor-mance	Score	8 Marathon Relay Perfor-mance	Score	Total score	Position
A																		
B																		
C																		
D																		
E																		

Curriculum Bank

PHYSICAL EDUCATION

Suggested layout for your sports day

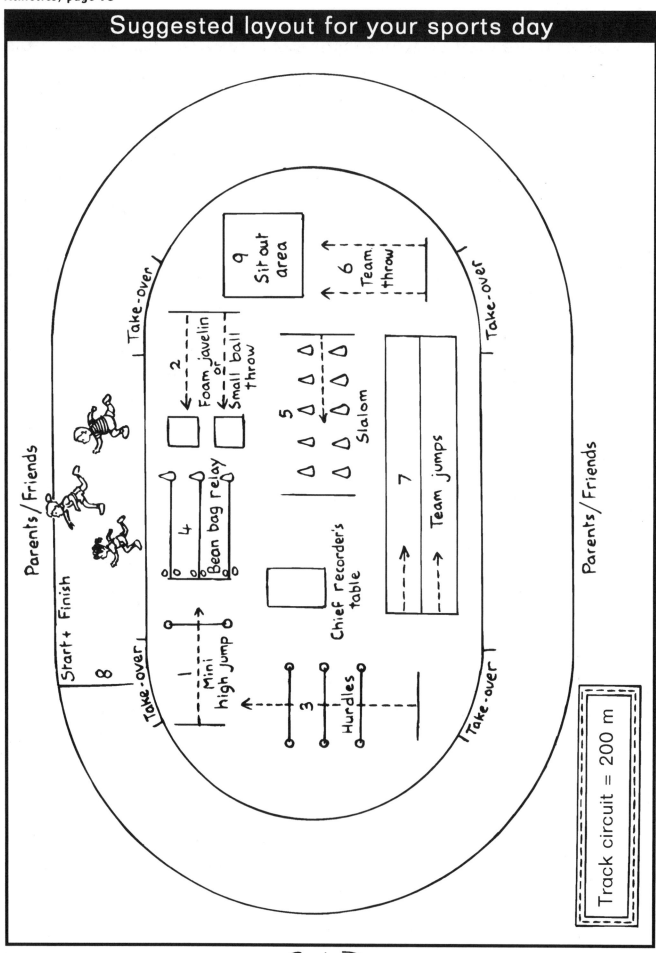

Start + Finish

Parents / Friends

Parents / Friends

Take-over

9
Sit out area

6
Team throw

2
Foam javelin or Small ball throw

5
Slalom

4
Bean bag relay

7
Team jumps

Chief Recorder's table

1
Mini high jump

8

3
Hurdles

Track circuit = 200 m

PHYSICAL EDUCATION

Photocopiables

Rules for individual events

1. Miniature Standing High Jump (jumping against the clock)

▲ Use a cane across two supports as a barrier.

▲ The objective in this event is for the team to clear the barrier as frequently as possible in 3 minutes, with the team members always jumping in a fixed order. The next jumper starts when the first has rounded the cone and recrossed the START line.

▲ A point is scored for each clearance: a single successful jump by a team member.

2. Foam Javelin Throw (throwing for accuracy)

▲ A 2m square is marked on the ground with the nearest edge 10m from the throwing line.

▲ Each team member has three throws and a point is scored every time the javelin lands within the square.

▲ If conditions are very windy, a tennis ball can be used instead of a foam javelin.

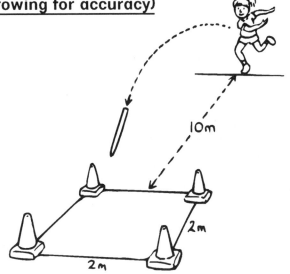

3. Hurdle Relay (hurdling)

▲ Three hurdles (a cane across two low supports) are arranged 6m apart, with a 9m run-in and a 9m run-out.

▲ The first team member runs across the hurdles to the end cone, goes round it and runs straight back (not over the hurdles) to the start line. The next runner starts. The event is timed. A knocked-down cane means the runner must start her/his leg again.

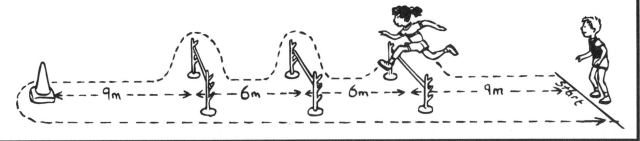

Curriculum Bank

PHYSICAL EDUCATION

Rules for individual events

4. Bean Bag Relay (running)

▲ Place two hoops 2m apart, with five bean bags in one hoop.

▲ The first team member moves the bean bags one at a time from one hoop to the other. Each bean bag has to be carried around the skittle. When all five have been transferred and the team member recrosses the start line, the next team member has the task of returning them in the same way to the original hoop.

▲ This process is repeated by all team members. The task is timed. (If the team has an odd number of members, it can finish the task with the bean bags in the second hoop.)

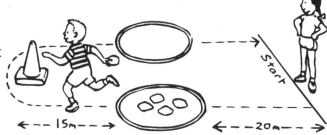

5. Slalom Relay (dribbling a football or hockey ball)

▲ Team members dribble a football (size 4), or dribble a tennis ball with a 'Unihoc' stick – whichever each runner prefers to use.

▲ Six cones are arranged 2 metres apart. The first runner starts and weaves in between the cones to cross the finish line. The ball is then picked up and carried back to the start line.

▲ The next runner then starts, and so on through the whole team. The event is timed.

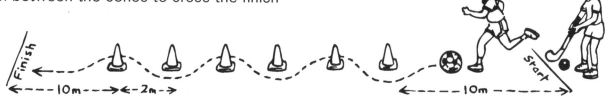

6. Team Throwing Event (throwing using a size 4 football)

▲ The football is thrown two-handed, as in a soccer throw-in.

▲ Each thrower is allowed 2 throws. The best throw is recorded for the team total distance.

PHYSICAL EDUCATION

Photocopiables

Rules for individual events

7. Team Jumping Event (standing broad jump)

▲ Team members line up one behind the other, behind a starting line. The first team member jumps and the landing point (where the heels come down) is marked with a cane.

▲ Each team member then proceeds to jump from the landing point of the previous jumper.

▲ Each team member completes three jumps. The total distance is measured.

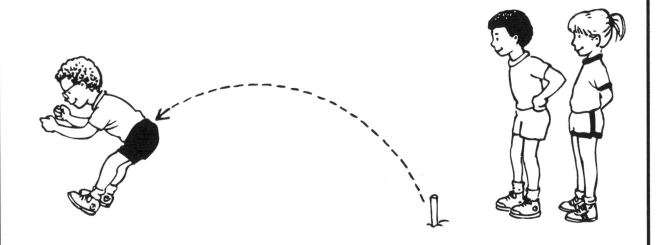

8. Six Lap Marathon (running)

▲ The team has to complete six laps of the 200m track as fast as possible. A relay baton is carried and passed from one runner to the next. Four change-over areas are marked on the track: the middle of each straight and bend.

▲ The running order of the total team must remain constant throughout – but how far each individual runs, and hence where on the circuit he/she will pass on the baton, is decided by the team in advance. However, a runner cannot run more than one complete lap or less than 100m at any one time. All change-overs must be made in the marked areas.

▲ The completion of the six laps is timed.

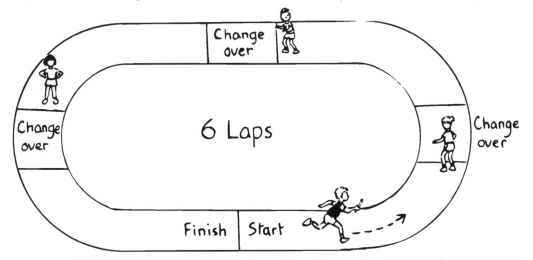

CurriculumBank

PHYSICAL EDUCATION

Outdoor and adventurous activities, page 79

Orienteering score card

Station	Code

Our team is (names)

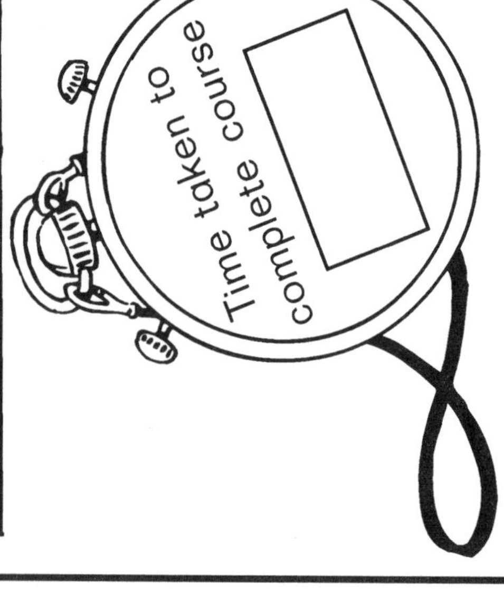

Time taken to complete course

Outdoor and adventurous activities, page 80

'Trust Walk'

The Scene

Your group has been temporarily blinded by a meteor storm – except your leader, who was lucky to have been wearing protective goggles. You have a difficult course to follow, but fortunately the route is marked by a length of rope tied to points along the path. The group must hold onto the rope and not let go. Your leader must safely guide the group – one at a time or one behind the other – along the rope trail by talking to them and warning them about changes in direction and obstacles in the way.

Each of you take a turn at being the sighted leader, while the rest of the group wear blindfolds.

You are not required to carry any equipment in this activity.

> **Equipment needed:**
> a light rope or string attached to posts, the ground (by pegs), trees and so on various obstacles

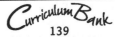
PHYSICAL
EDUCATION

'Escape the Fire'

The Scene

You are surrounded by a forest fire and your only means of escape is **through** a narrow tunnel (the suspended hoop). Your group – together with all of your equipment – must move through the tunnel in order to escape the raging inferno. You must **not** dive through. Remember that your equipment is very important to you and needs to be handled carefully.

Equipment needed:
a hoop suspended
in a goalmouth
2 light 5' planks
1 small tyre

PHYSICAL
EDUCATION

Outdoor and adventurous activities, page 80

'Crossing the Poisonous Swamp'

The Scene

Your group has arrived at a poisonous swamp (marked by two rows of skittles or cones). You cannot go around it, but to put one foot in it means certain death. You have carried certain items of equipment with you which may be helpful in allowing you to cross the swamp safely.

Equipment needed:
skittles/cones
2 light 5' planks
1 small tyre

30m

Score Card

Name _____   **Date** _____

<u>S</u>pider's <u>Web</u>

Time

<u>M</u>ap <u>M</u>emory

Map A   matches   Map

Map B   matches   Map

Map C   matches   Map

Map D   matches   Map

Time

<u>R</u>adioactive <u>B</u>eanbags

Time

Total time _____   **Position** _____

**PHYSICAL
EDUCATION**

My Journey Log

Name _____ **Date** _____

Date of journey _____

From _____ To _____

Planned departure time _____

Estimated time of arrival (ETA) _____

Actual departure time _____ Actual arrival time _____

Weather forecast _____

Actual weather _____

Distance kilometres _____

My food for the journey _____

_____

My clothes for the journey _____

_____

Footwear _____

_____

I will look for the following landmarks   1. _____

2. _____   3. _____

▲ Draw them on the back of this sheet if you can.

PHYSICAL
EDUCATION

Things to observe

Name _____   **Date** _____

I will look for these plants:

1 _____

2 _____

3 _____

▲ Can you draw them?

I will look for these trees:

1 _____

2 _____

3 _____

▲ Can you draw them?

I will look for these animals and birds:

1 _____

2 _____

3 _____

4 _____

5 _____

▲ Can you draw them?

PHYSICAL EDUCATION

Outdoor and adventurous activities, page 83

The Country Code Quiz

Name _____   **Date** _____

The Country Code tells us how we ought to behave and
things to remember when we are visiting the country.

▲ Try to fill in the missing words

'Keep to the _____ across farmland.'

'Fasten all _____ '

'Avoid f_____ '

'Leave no _____ – take it home.'

'Safeguard w_____ supplies.'

'Go carefully on country _____ '

'Keep _____ under control.'

'Avoid damaging w_____ and f_____ '

'Protect _____ '

Why do you think these rules are important?

_____

_____

_____

▲ Now choose one of these rules and design your own poster to illustrate it.
It can be funny or serious, but remember that it must get the message across!

Floating and Sculling

MUSHROOM FLOAT

Tucked shape, chin on chest.
Legs bent with knees towards
chest.
Arms held loosely around shins.
The body floats with the back
out of the water.

STAR FLOAT

On the back:
Take a deep breath.
Lie still.
Extend the arms and legs into a star shape.

On the front:
Take a deep breath.
Submerge face in water and lie still.
Extend the arms and legs into a star shape.

SCULLING

Hand action is figure
of eight.
Keep fingers together
and hands cupped.
Keep hands below
the water at hip level.
Make movements as
smooth as possible.

Swimming, pages 93 and 97

Water Survival

H.E.L.P. POSITION

Remain motionless to conserve energy.
Keep legs together.
Elbows close to sides, hands holding
collar of life-jacket.
Keep back against the waves.

If there is no life-jacket, any floating
object can be used. Try to take up
H.E.L.P. position while holding onto it.

HUDDLE

A group of people can huddle together to
reduce collective heat loss.
Allow legs to find a comfortable position.
Put arms around the waist or shoulders of
those on either side.

If life-jackets are not being worn, then the
huddle can be made using any large floating
object that will support the group. Stay
motionless to keep the group balanced.

PHYSICAL
EDUCATION

Swimming, pages 94 and 98

Front Crawl

1 Body position horizontal. Head in line with body.

2 Legs pass as close as possible to each other, without touching.

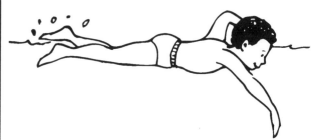

3 Head begins to turn.

4 Head completes turn. Breathe in.

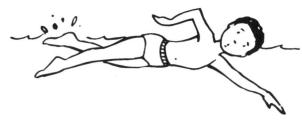

5 Head starts to turn back.

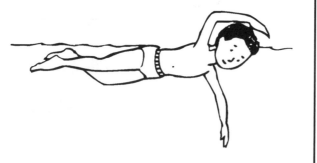

6 Head completes turn. Breathe out.

Basic arm action is continuous and alternate, and provides the main propulsion.

Basic leg action is an alternating up and down movement.

PHYSICAL
EDUCATION

Swimming, pages 90, 94 and 98

Breast Stroke

Body position should be
as horizontal as possible.

As the arms pull down, the
legs should remain trailing
and streamlined.

Arms begin to recover
and legs prepare to kick.

Arms recover, legs
thrust backwards.

Horizontal body position
on completion of stroke.

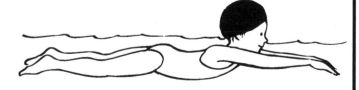

RHYTHM
Pull, Breathe, Kick, Glide.

PHYSICAL
EDUCATION

Swimming, pages 89, 91, 94, 95 and 98

Back Crawl

1 Body position horizontal. Back of head in the water.

2 Body stretched with legs and feet extended.

3 Knees remain below the water surface.

4 Toes just break the water surface.

5 Little finger enters the water first.

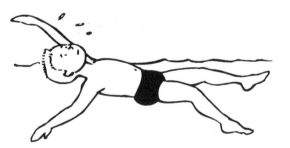

6 Arm entry passes close to the ear.

Basic arm action is continuous and alternate. One arm enters the water as the other is extended close to the hip.

Basic leg action is an alternating up and down movement.

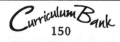

PHYSICAL
EDUCATION

Swimming, page 98

Butterfly

1 Body position as near to horizontal as possible.	
2 Arms enter water extended, approximately in line with the shoulders, hands pointing down.	
3 Pull and push action of the arms making a 'keyhole' shape under the water.	
4 Leg action balances the movements of the arms and upper body.	
5 Leg action from the hips, push down hard and keep action continuous. Keep legs together.	
Pattern of arm action under the water.	ENTRY · · · EXIT

Arm action is the main propulsive force.
Movements are simultaneous and continuous.

Leg action is upwards and downwards. Both legs move simultaneously.

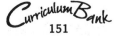

PHYSICAL EDUCATION

Assessment and record-keeping, page 100

Physical Education

Class Recording Sheet

Class _____ Year _____

Name	Games				Gym		Dance		Swimming			Athletics			O/A		General requirements		Planning skills		Evaluation skills		
	a	b	c	d	e	f	g	h	i	j	k	l	m	n	o	p	q	r	s	t	u	v	w	x

Assessment and record-keeping, page 100

Key

Games
a. Sending (passing, striking a ball)
b. Receiving (catching, controlling a ball)
c. Travelling (moving with a ball)
d. Team play (knowledge and understanding of rules and tactics)

Gymnastics
e. Individual skills (control, poise and technique)
f. Sequence building (fluency and imagination)

Dance
g. Compositional skills (constructing the dance)
h. Expression (interpreting the dance stimulus effectively)

Swimming
i. Ability to swim 25 metres
j. Stroke technique
k. Knowledge and understanding of water safety

Athletics
l. Running
m. Jumping
n. Throwing

Outdoor/Adventurous activities
o. Problem solving
p. Navigational skills

General requirements
q. Knowledge and understanding of the health benefits of exercise
r. Knowledge and understanding of safe practice in physical education
s. Attitude and social skills

Planning skills
t. Ability to explore tasks set
u. Ability to select movement actions or responses

Evaluation skills
v. Ability to recognise actions
u. Ability to describe actions
x. Ability to compare and contrast actions

Grading
1 = Working below expectations
2 = Working in line with expectations
3 = Working beyond expectations

Teacher annual record sheet

National Curriculum
Physical Education Key Stage 2   Year Group ———

Class ———

Please indicate the types of activity you have covered with your class/year group under the headings below.

Term	Gymnastics	Dance	Games	Athletics	Outdoor and adventurous activity	Swimming

PHYSICAL
EDUCATION

Teacher self-evaluation sheet

Criteria for evaluating the physical education lesson

1. Did the lesson(s) improve skill levels throughout the class?

_____

_____

2. Were the activities presented appropriate for all pupils?

_____

_____

3. Were the activities demanding enough to enhance previous fitness levels?

_____

_____

4. Were the teaching styles employed effective in promoting pupil learning?

_____

_____

5. What opportunities were provided to develop responsibility and initiative among pupils?

_____

_____

6. How much attention was paid to safe practice and the establishment of a safe working environment?

_____

_____

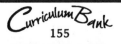

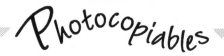

Merit awards (1)

(Name)

BRONZE

merit award for

(activity)

in
(PE)

Signed

(Name)

BRONZE

merit award for

(activity)

in
(PE)

Signed

(Name)

BRONZE

merit award for

(activity)

in
(PE)

Signed

(Name)

SILVER

merit award for

(activity)

in
(PE)

Signed

(Name)

SILVER

merit award for

(activity)

in
(PE)

Signed

(Name)

SILVER

merit award for

(activity)

in
(PE)

Signed

(Name)

GOLD

merit award for

(activity)

in
(PE)

Signed

(Name)

GOLD

merit award for

(activity)

in
(PE)

Signed

(Name)

GOLD

merit award for

(activity)

in
(PE)

Signed

PHYSICAL EDUCATION

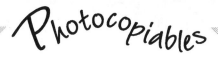
Merit awards (2)

(Name)

BRONZE
merit award for

(Personal effort)

in
(PE)

Signed

(Name)

BRONZE
merit award for

(Personal effort)

in
(PE)

Signed

(Name)

BRONZE
merit award for

(Personal effort)

in
(PE)

Signed

(Name)

SILVER
merit award for

(Personal effort)

in
(PE)

Signed

(Name)

SILVER
merit award for

(Personal effort)

in
(PE)

Signed

(Name)

SILVER
merit award for

(Personal effort)

in
(PE)

Signed

(Name)

GOLD
merit award for

(Personal effort)

in
(PE)

Signed

(Name)

GOLD
merit award for

(Personal effort)

in
(PE)

Signed

(Name)

GOLD
merit award for

(Personal effort)

in
(PE)

Signed

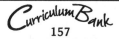
PHYSICAL EDUCATION

INFORMATION TECHNOLOGY WITHIN PE AT KEY STAGE 2

The essentials of physical education

Children can keep records of their exercise or fitness levels, using simple computer spreadsheets, databases, and graphing packages to store, retrieve and present information.

A simple spreadsheet can be set up using the same format as photocopiable page 104. It could be set up in advance so that it works out the total for the week automatically. Children can save their own spreadsheet file and add information daily, retrieving and resaving the file as they work. The graphical options could also be used to display the information, for example in a table. The spreadsheet could also be set up with different columns showing different types of exercise. It could even be extended to contain all of the class data on one sheet, with different sections for different children.

Similar records could also be kept on a database, with each record identifying different activities for a specific day. Each child could have her/his own database file and record the different types of exercise over a period of a week or longer. At the end of the specified time, the children could total the different types of exercise or display the results graphically. Suggest that they find out when most exercise took place, or whether girls took more exercise than boys.

Where they are required to take pulse measurements, children can be introduced to simple computer monitoring activities – such as using a pulse meter, which clips onto the ear lobe or fits over the finger and gives a digital readout of the pulse rate. These sensors can be connected to the computer and, using appropriate software, graphs can be drawn showing how the pulse rate changes with exercise.

If children are involved in research about their bodies, information can be obtained from encyclopaedia CD-ROMs or from more interactive dedicated titles such as the Dorling Kindersley *Ultimate Human Body*.

Games

Activities which require children to confirm, develop or invent rules for games provide a good context for developing skills in creating, organising and presenting information.

Working in their teams, children can use a word processor or desktop publishing package to write the rules for the games they have created. Demonstrate how the *'cut and paste'* or *'drag and drop'* facilities can be used to move blocks of text around so that information can be placed in the correct sequence. If the games are played over a series of lessons, children can save and then retrieve their files and edit, amend or rewrite the rules as the games evolve.

Once the rules have been completed, the groups will need to decide how they are going to present them. Demonstrate how to use formatting commands such as centre,

justification, tabs and hanging indents to lay out work. Children should also be shown how to select suitable fonts and font sizes to present their work. The children's rules can be printed out and added to a class compendium.

This work can be extended by adding illustrations – for example, of the equipment needed, the layout of the playing pitch or strategic moves. They could be drawn using an art or drawing package, or scanned from the children's own line art and then imported into the word processor.

A more adventurous approach would be for the groups to create a presentation of their game using multimedia authoring software such as *Magpie* or *Hyperstudio*. Music can be sampled from an audio CD-ROM, composed with music software or recorded using a microphone attached to the computer. Children's voices can be recorded in the same way and used as a commentary. Illustrations created with art and drawing packages, or taken from commercial clip art, can be added. It is even possible to use pictures of the game in progress scanned from photographs, taken with a digital camera or digitised from video pictures.

A typical presentation could start with a title page containing a contents list. When the user clicks with the mouse on, for example, 'rules', he/she is taken to a set of pages which outline the rules of the game. Forward and back arrows will take the user to other linked pages.

Gymnastics

Children can use the computer to extend, develop and communicate ideas developed during gymnastic activities.

Pairs or groups could use an art or drawing package to record the shapes, movements or sequences they have developed. Simple stick people can easily be drawn using the line drawing facilities of a drawing or art package, setting lines of varying thickness and showing joints. Copies of the basic shape can be made by cutting and pasting them on to the drawing area or using the duplicate command.

If the children use a drawing package, the limbs on the basic shape can be altered to create the shapes made during the lesson. These can be built into tableaux of the sequences created. More able or adventurous pupils could experiment with an animation package such as *Noot* in which the shapes can be linked together to form a simple animation.

Other shape work, such as symmetrical and balanced paired work, can also be explored. Demonstrate how to make symmetrical shapes by copying the original shape and then 'flipping' it to a symmetrical position. Children could also design their own apparatus layouts to accompany the sequences. To undertake this work, the children will need to know how to create shapes, copy and resize them, and rotate and move them around the drawing area. If a drawing package is used, make sure the children know how to alter the lines and to link shapes together to make a single object.

Some of the sequence work could also be used to develop children's use of the word processor to organise and

PHYSICAL EDUCATION

structure work: jumbled-up instructions could be saved as a file, retrieved by the children and reordered to the correct sequence. This will give children an opportunity to use the *'cut and paste'* or *'drag and drop'* facilities of the word processor to move text into the correct position.

Children could also use a video camera to record the work of other children. Still images from this or a digital camera could be used to give a presentation on the work carried out: pictures taken could be imported into a word processor, where a suitable caption could be added. Such pictures could be used to make a class display or book on safe practice.

Dance

A computer can be used to record and present various aspects of the work undertaken in the dance activities.

The children can use a word processor to write instructions for their dance. Alternatively, they could use an art or drawing package, representing a dance step as a simple footprint shape which can be copied to mark out the pattern of steps. Arrows to indicate changes of direction could be drawn using the arrowhead option for lines or imported from a clip art collection. The children will need to be shown how to draw or import a footprint, duplicate it, move it and rotate it.

If the facilities are available, some children may be able to animate the dance steps using a multimedia authoring package. The dance steps could be set up to show the dance sequence in time to the music, which can be recorded as a sound sample from the CD-ROM and incorporated into the software. An alternative approach would be to use a digitised video sequence to show the dance on the computer screen.

Athletics

A computer can be used to record, present and analyse the results of the different athletic activities.

Set the athletics photocopiable sheet up on a computer database with a single record for each child. The fieldnames can be set up in the same manner. It might be interesting to have a gender field so that possible differences between boys and girls can be explored. Children can enter the data over a period of time, saving and retrieving it as necessary. Make sure that regular backups of the data file are made.

Once the data has been input, children should be encouraged to interrogate it and look for patterns (such as whether faster long-distance runners are faster sprinters). The graphical facilities can be used to present the information in different ways and statistical functions used to find the mean distance thrown or the range in the class.

The scoring from the sports day could also be done using a simple spreadsheet with a row for each team and a column for each event. The scores from the judges could be entered for each event. An adjacent column could be used to work out the teams' positions. These can be totalled automatically across each row to find the winning team. The spreadsheet could also be used to find the average times or scores.

Outdoor and adventurous activities

A number of software packages exist which assist children's ability to read and use maps at different scales. Some, such as Sherston Software's *Map Venture,* help children learn about maps and also provide an adventure game; others provide a range of maps and exercises of varying difficulty.

The children could also plan out their own routes over simple maps using a ROAMER. A floor map of the school site could be created with 30cm grid squares. Children can then programme the ROAMER to move around the map to different locations. Older children could produce similar maps and routes using the turtle graphics part of LOGO.

Children could use a word processor to write letters home about a forthcoming trip. Create a template file with a list of headings to ensure all the important information is included. This can then be saved on to a disk so that the children can retrieve it and use it as the basis for their own letter. Demonstrate how to format the address using appropriate commands. A shorter exercise would be to design an information card giving facts about the trip.

The children could produce their own expedition guide using the knowledge they have gained and information researched from other sources. They could work in groups; food, clothing, route, survival tips, weather lore, and so on could form different sections of the guide, which could finally be printed and presented as a class book.

An alternative project would be for the children to write a trip diary using a word processor. Groups or individual children could write about a part of the walk and include illustrations drawn with an art package, scanned from their own line drawings or photographs or taken using a digital camera. An extension of this would be to make a multimedia presentation using an authoring package which combines text, pictures and children's recorded speech.

Swimming

Children can create their own water safety posters (focusing on poolside safety and behaviour or safety near ice or at the seaside or rivers) using a word processor or desktop publishing package. Illustrations could be imported from an art package or clipart, or scanned from line drawings and photographs. Text can be added, fonts selected and other effects included to create the poster. Alternatively the whole poster could be created using an art or drawing package.

Children could use CD-ROM encyclopaedias or the Internet to search for other information about water safety, buoyancy or hypothermia. Pictures and text could be imported into a word processor, edited and then presented as a survival guide or booklet on the topic selected.

Children could also use a word processor or desktop publishing package to create their own stroke guides based on the work at the pool. These could be presented as a class book or developed into a multimedia presentation using authoring software.

IT links

The grids on this page relate the activities in this book to specific areas of IT and to relevant software resources. The software listed is a selection of programs generally available to primary schools and is not intended as a recommended list.

GRID 1

AREA OF IT	SOFTWARE	CHAP 1	CHAP 2	CHAP 3	CHAP 4	CHAP 5	CHAP 6	CHAP 7
Communicating Information	Word Processor		✓	✓	✓		✓	✓
Communicating Information	DTP		✓		✓			✓
Communicating Information	Art		✓	✓	✓			✓
Communicating Information	Drawing software		✓	✓				✓
Communicating Information	Authoring software		✓		✓			
Communicating Information	CD-ROM	✓					✓	✓
Communicating Information	Authoring software		✓		✓		✓	✓
Handling information	Graphing software	✓				✓		
Handling information	Database	✓				✓		
Handling information	Spreadsheet	✓				✓		
Monitoring	Data Logging	✓						
Control	Roamer/LOGO						✓	

GRID 2

SOFTWARE TYPE	BBC/MASTER	RISCOS	NIMBUS/186	WINDOWS	MACINTOSH
Word Processor	Pendown Folio	Pendown Desk Top Folio TextEase	All Write Write On	Word for Windows Kid Works 2 Creative Writer	Kid Works 2 Easy Works Creative Writer
DTP	Front Page Extra	Desk Top Folio Pendown DTP TextEase	Front Page Extra NewSPAper	Creative Writer NewSPAper	Creative Writer
Drawing Software		Draw Vector Art Works		Claris Works Oak Draw	Claris Works
Art Package	Image	1st Paint Kid Pix Splash	PaintSpa	Colour Magic Kid Pix 2 Fine Artist	Kid Pix 2 Flying Colours Fine Artist
Multi-media Authoring		Magpie Hyperstudio Genesis		Genesis Hyperstudio Illuminus	Hyperstudio
Spreadsheet	Grasshopper Pigeonhole	Grasshopper Advantage Key Count	Grasshopper	Excel Starting Grid Claris Works Sparks	Claris Works
Database	Grass	Junior Pinpoint Find IT KeyNote	Grass	Sparks Claris Works Information Workshop	Claris Works Easy Works
Graphing Software	Datashow	Graph IT Data Plot	Datagraph	Datagraph Easy Works	Easy Works
Data Logging	Sense-it	Junior Insight	Investigate	Insight Investigate	Insight
CD-ROM		Children's Micropaedia Hutchinson Oxford Junior		Encarta 96 Children's Micropaedia Grolier	Encarta 96 Grolier

PHYSICAL
EDUCATION